Developing Quality Schools

This book is produced as a small tribute to the partnership of all those working to provide quality teaching and quality learning in schools throughout the shires of Hereford and Worcester, England.

Developing Quality Schools

Edited by

Colin Bayne-Jardine
and
Peter Holly

 The Falmer Press

(A member of the Taylor & Francis Group)
London • Washington, D.C.

UK   The Falmer Press, 4 John St, London WC1N 2ET
USA   The Falmer Press, Taylor & Francis Inc., 1900 Frost Road, Suite 101,
           Bristol, PA 19007

First published 1994

A catalogue record of this publication is available from the British Library
ISBN 07507 0242 7 cased
ISBN 07507 0243 5 paper

Library of Congress Cataloging-in-Publication Data are available on request

Jacket design by Caroline Archer

Typeset in 11/13pt Bembo by
Graphicraft Typesetters Ltd., Hong Kong

Printed in Great Britain by Burgess Science Press, Basingstoke on paper which has a specified pH value on final paper manufacture of not less than 7.5 and is therefore 'acid free'.

Contents

Introduction

The educational system in England and Wales is in a state of flux. Centralisation (control by central government) is increasing at the same time as local power is being decentralised to the schools. The semi-autonomous school, long vaunted by many change theorists, is fast becoming a reality. What this all means is that the Local Education Authority (LEA) is in danger of being squeezed out in this new scenario of centralised decentralisation — unless, of course, the LEA can re-create itself and discover a new role as a service operation. In the USA, school districts, faced with the same changing situation, are rapidly adopting a 'customer service orientation' under the influence of Total Quality Management (TQM) and the writings of Tom Peters (1989) and his exhortation (echoed by Charles Handy in the UK) to get 'close to the customer'.

Hereford and Worcester LEA has been quietly adapting to this revolution. With 'service' replacing 'control' and horizontalism taking over from verticalism, it was appreciated that the nascent local partnership required 'systemic congruence' (Holly, 1991) in order to avoid dissonance and therefore loss of potential and impact. With these understandings in mind the local inspectorate has been changing policies and practices to suit the new deal. The Authority's inspection and review work, its teacher appraisal schemes and, above all, its inservice development and support services have all been geared to the needs of the self-developing, self-managing and self-reviewing school (see Holly and Southworth, 1989; Caldwell and Spinks, 1989; and Bayne-Jardine, 1991). As Principal Inspector of Schools in the Authority, Colin Bayne-Jardine has spear-headed these changes. All the other contributors to this book have also been involved either directly or indirectly with the changes as internal or external change agents. Peter Holly has been working for the Authority and its schools as an independent consultant and, in a very real sense, this present volume is a sequel to Holly's earlier book, *The Developing School* which he co-authored with Geoff Southworth. This book is the story of one LEA's real attempt to grasp the future by encouraging the schools to reconnoitre the work of relative autonomy (decentralisation), while wrestling with the plethora of centralised change mandates and, at the same time, keeping faith with the principles of self-development and self-actualization. This is a most delicate balancing act and, increasingly, LEAs will have to walk the tightrope of having to retain the trust of more independent, assertive schools on the one hand and a more aggressive, demanding central government on the other. This book depicts the first faltering steps of one Local Education Authority as it steps out across the high-wire.

1   Supporting Self-Developing Schools

Colin Bayne-Jardine

> It is true that we shall never reach the goal; it is even more than
> probable there is no such place; and if we lived for centuries
> and were endowed with the powers of a god, we should find
> ourselves not much nearer what we wanted at the end. O toil-
> ing hands of mortals! O unwearied feet, travelling ye know not
> whither! Soon, soon, it seems to you, you must come forth on
> some conspicuous hilltop, and but a little way further, against
> the setting sun, descry the spires of El Dorado. Little do you
> know your own blessedness; for to travel hopefully is a better
> thing than to arrive, and the true success is to labour. Robert
> Louis Stevenson, *El Dorado*, 1879

All administrators know the temptation to tidy up an organisation so
that they can claim that El Dorado has been reached. Yet, tne reality
is that schools will only change and develop if the teachers within the
institutions are empowered to develop themselves. Schools are living
organisations and cannot be forced into a tight organisation and or-
dered to develop. Yet some structure and support is necessary if self-
evaluation is to be more than introspection. We all need the critical
friend to ensure that a review is purposeful and rigorous.

1

Whilst an audit of a school's performance is valuable and indeed necessary, it is not sufficient to help a school to develop. The Office of

Standards in Education (Ofsted) *Framework for the Inspection of Schools* (1992) provides a thorough and detailed review of a school's performance at the time of the inspection. The governors are required to respond to the report with an action plan and it is at this point that most schools will need the help of a professional adviser. The self-developing school is not the self-sufficient school. The role of the critical friend is vital. Writing in 1985 Eisner had this to say:

> Teachers are too close; **a critical friend** provides a fresh eye, distance and an illuminative intent. Trust is crucial for a meaningful dialogue between teacher and critic; this is not quite coaching, more a counsel of friends . . . one makes oneself vulnerable only to those who one believes are not intending to hurt. Joint reflection rests on the investment of time in the classroom and an integrated process of professional development.

Handy (1989) concurs on the importance of attracting the support of mentors. Learning organisations, he says, need mentors and mentoring. Therefore,

> The mentor role will become increasingly important . . . Properly selfish individuals will, if they are wise, look for their own mentors. Organisations could make this easier by maintaining a list of approved, and paid for, mentors, inside and outside. They will not always be people in great authority, those mentors, and will seldom be one's immediate superior. Mentoring is a skill on its own. Quiet people have it more than loud people; for mentors are able to live vicariously, getting pleasure from the success of others; they are interpreters not theorists, nor action men; best perhaps in the reflective stage of learning, people who are attracted by influence not power.

Such people are much more process consultants than external evaluators. Indeed, Holly (1990) has included **critical friends** as one of his 'Six Cs of Organisational Development'. Such consultants for school-based development and evaluation are critical friends and mentors who bring their external perspectives to bear on internal matters. They are there to add to the evaluation work not to detract from it. It is their perspectives and their insights that are needed, not their control.

Indeed, while involvement in self-evaluation (as part of school-based development) not only contributes to the process of internalisation (ie. growth from within) but also encourages the transfer of ownership to those who are internal to the school, and the mobilisation and energising of their collective efforts, it is important to widen the concept of self-evaluation to include 'external' critical friends. If internal development demands internal/self-evaluation, both are considerably enhanced through the application of an external perspective. Collaborative inquiry, therefore, can be conducted amongst those who are internal to the situation and between those who are both internal and external. It may well be the case that any analysis of the culture of the school (through an approach such as **portraiture**) is dependent on the incorporation of an external perspective. Critical friends are vital for any inquiry to be genuinely collaborative. Educational administrators can promote a living social system's self-renewal. They can provide the vital input to create a nucleus of change. The major task is to create an organisational climate in which the self-managing, self-reviewing and self-developing school can flourish. In the UK, the task is complicated by the conflicting messages from central government. On the one hand, schools in England and Wales are obliged by Act of Parliament to deliver the National Curriculum, while, on the other hand, they are being given power to manage themselves under the local management scheme. The Local Education Authority has to find a strategy to harmonise expectations from central government and from the schools. The true success must indeed be to labour!

The first task has been to provide organisational clarity. The model for development is not static. It is constantly moving and changing. Within a cosmological map (Figure 1.1) which should be shared with all headteachers, every institution produces its own development plan. These plans are the focus for the work of outside agencies and are used to identify institutional training needs. Here again a balance must be kept between the tight control of a standard model for development and the loose rein of leaving all schools to carry out their own planning process. It is quite clear that teachers need a framework within which to work provided that they feel able to influence the nature of that framework as their confidence in the process increases. Industry has shown that organisational culture can be changed. General Electric has shown that an attack on bureaucracy, followed by a strategy involving the group's workforce and customers more actively in the way the business is run, can bring a climate change. The process is difficult and El Dorado will not be reached only seen ahead. The vision is vital to the enterprise.

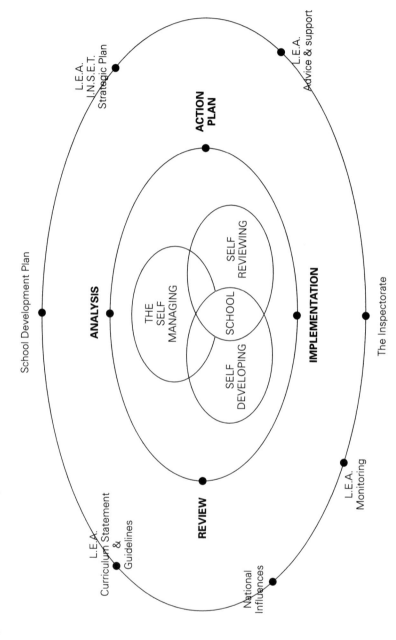

Figure 1.1   A model for development

2

It seems most appropriate when analysing the system that learns, to start with a quotation from Alfred North Whitehead, the Anglo-American philosopher, mathematician and educationalist. This quotation comes from Whitehead's *Aims of Education*, first published in 1932, yet, it can be argued, so relevant today.

> After all, our pupils are alive, and cannot be chopped into separate bits, like the pieces of a jig-saw puzzle. In the production of a mechanism the constructive energy lies outside it, and adds discrete parts to discrete parts. The case is far different for a living organism which grows by its own impulse towards self-development. This impulse can be stimulated and guided from outside the organism, and it can also be killed. But for all your stimulation and guidance the creative impulse towards growth comes from within, and is intensely characteristic of the individual . . . what I am now insisting is that the principle of progress is from within: the discovery is made by ourselves, the discipline is self-discipline, and the function is the outcome of our own initiative.

While Whitehead is talking here about student learning, he is talking about some generic principles of learning, organisational learning (see Senge, 1990). In *The Developing School* (Holly and Southworth, 1989) — ie. the school that maximises student learning and that can itself be called a learning organisation — learning is what everyone does, students and teachers alike.

Moreover, when the principles built into the Whitehead quotation are applied at the level of organisational change and learning (see Handy, 1989) they demand the following:

(i)   a systemic, holistic, coherent, and integrated approach, which avoids the fragmentation of being 'chopped into separate bits';

(ii) the avoidance of a mechanistic approach which is both bolt-on, additive, arbitrary and unco-ordinated in nature and which retains the 'constructive energy' outside the learning organisation;

(iii) the promotion of an organic approach which treats the learning organisation as a 'living organism which grows by its own impulse towards self-development'. According to Holly and Southworth (1989), the developing school is the self-developing school. The learning school is a self-developing, self-reviewing, self-knowing, self-regulating, self-determining, self-renewing organism; it is alive with potential;

(iv)   the provision of sympathetic/empathetic external support which guides, facilitates and enhances the learning of the organisation and which stimulates growth rather than stifles it. Ownership of, and commitment to learning have to flourish inside the organisation, which is why, according to Senge (1990), so many ill-conceived interventions are not just ineffective but also 'addictive', 'in the sense of fostering increased dependency and lessened abilities of local people to solve their own problems';

(v)   the release of the 'creative impulse towards growth' that 'comes from within' and which is learner/learning school-specific and needs-based, ie. 'intensely characteristic of the individual'. Different learning organisations, like different students, have different learning needs. Differentiation, therefore, is a key concept;

(vi)   the acceptance of the principle that 'progress is from within'. What Holly (1990) has referred to as internalisation reflects the 'inside-outness' of this perspective. It is intra-ventionist rather than interventionist; it is more about learning than teaching.

Taking these six points together, Whitehead is saying much about learning and change, growth and development. Indeed, as Handy (1989) has observed:

Change, after all, is only another word for growth, another synonym for learning . . . learning is not finding out what other people already know, but is solving our own problems for our own purposes, by questioning, thinking and testing until the solution is a new part of our life . . . A learning organisation needs to have a formal way of asking questions, seeking out theories, testing them and reflecting upon them.

Learning, in this sense, is about what Schon (1987) has called 'reflection-in-action'; it is about action research (ie. action-oriented research and research-based action) and on-going reflection and self-evaluation. It is action-learning. And as Senge (1990), Handy (1989) and Timar and Kirp (1987) have all emphasised, the practice of change and learning has to be capacity-enhancing in order to extend what Timar and Kirp call 'institutional competence'. In other words, in doing supported development and evaluation now, we must be enabled to learn from the practice in order to do them better — for ourselves — next time round. Indeed, the concept of capacity-building operates on two levels. For instance, evaluating our developments can not only increase our capacity to perform well in those areas of development but also further our capacity to do better evaluation. This concept of dual enhancement is akin to what Argyris and Schon (1978) have referred to as single and double loop learning. They argue that most organisations can accomplish single-loop learning in solving everyday problems. They further contend, however, that for significant organisational development and for ensuring long-term survival and renewal, change must occur in more fundamental ways. Although problems must be solved in a single loop, new ways of learning how to solve problems must be learned as well, thus adding another loop to the learning cycle — what they refer to as 'double loop learning'. The best evaluation practice, therefore, should enable those inside an organisation to both learn and to learn about learning/to learn how to learn. Bawden (1989), in building on the work of Kolb and Argyris and Schon, has depicted what he calls 'reflective experiential practice'.

While the level of single-loop learning is fundamental (Argyris and Schon stress that all those in the organisation should be involved in detecting and correcting 'errors' — this is what makes for effectiveness, thus enabling the organisation to achieve its goals) double-loop learning is more radical — and essential for restructuring. Argyris and Schon maintain that there has to be an in-depth investigation of the nested organisational norms regarding how inquiries are conducted in the school/how the organisation learns.

This, they say, is not a case of doing things better but doing them differently. Thus different strategies are adopted and, in so doing, the norms of inquiry are questioned. This is the level of learning about learning. It is close to what Bateson has called 'deutero-learning' and is essential if the organisation is to learn how to restructure itself and its culture, to reflect on what facilitates and inhibits learning and to invent and evaluate strategies for learning. In summary, then, the process of evaluation must always be an educative, learning experience with the evaluator — whether an insider or an outsider — being the facilitator of learning.

The role of the Local Education Authority and any outside body must be to provide such vision and develop a working relationship which encourages teachers to embark together on the developmental process. This process is given clarity and purpose by the format of a county development plan. Data-gathering is the first step in this process so that perceptions of the school 'as it is now' are clarified. The ultimate purpose of data-gathering, reflection and dialogue is action and teachers are encouraged to take action in collaborative groups. The critical friend can empower teachers by questioning, by coaching, and by encouraging. The purpose of the model for development is to give teachers the security of a framework within which they can take charge of their own development with the intention of improving the quality of teaching and learning in all schools.

This book has grown out of the attempt to encourage and support quality development in one English shire county. A team gathered to discuss the evaluation of the process and from this meeting came the idea that it would be useful to set down the way in which an attempt was made to provide a coherent strategy to support quality schools. There is plenty of evidence that schools only develop effectively if they are fully involved in any development. The move towards the local management of schools has created a need to work out a new form of partnership and this is a description of one group travelling hopefully together.

2   Discovering the Six Cs

Peter Holly

The LEA can be a learning system. In order to merit such a title, however, at each of the organisation levels (the LEA, the school and the classroom) there has to be a system for learning. Action research can provide this. It is from the recent work on action research that the '6 Cs' have emerged. These six 'Criteria for Success' all happen to start with the letter 'C'. But more about that later in this chapter.

> She's second nature to me now,
> Like breathing out and breathing in
> (from *My Fair Lady*)

> Looking at what we're doing should become as natural as breathing.
>   (School co-ordinator)

In the last ten years, on both sides of the Atlantic, action research has come a long way (see Holly, 1989 and 1991(a) and (b)). In the early 1980s it was in danger of being backed — by its erstwhile protagonists — into a self-contained, doctrinaire and self-indulgent corner. It had become a counter-culture; a distinctive sub-culture rather than a part of the culture; a side-stream rather than the main-stream. Perhaps this was to be expected. Large, and even small, schools were fast becoming bureaucratic, hierarchical and dehumanised (see Holly, 1984). Action research stands for the antithesis of these things. It is democratic and humane in spirit; participative, open and flexible in character. It is, essentially, about learning; it is also about empowerment. Above all, it stands for the internalisation of the change process (see Holly, 1990).

But ten years ago these things went against the grain. Yet, ten years on, a significant turn-about has occurred. Action research is no longer the 'enfant terrible'. No doubt action research itself has changed somewhat, but so have the schools as organisations in which action research is fast becoming embedded. Undoubtedly, it has been a period of integration, even implosion. Evaluation theory has changed enough for action research to be countenanced. Change theory has changed and, crucially, so has organisational theory (see Sirotnik, 1989). Moveover, learning theory has been included, thus adding to the potency of the mix. But it is the chemistry of the mixture that is all-important and it is this mixing with which schools are currently experimenting.

As I have pointed out elsewhere (Holly, 1989), action research may have lost its name only to gain long overdue success and recognition — as a vital, built-in component of the internalised processing of change in schools. As one teacher observed to me recently, 'change is an internal thing; it comes from the inside'. Given the process of implosion, however, no one element of the package remains distinctive and independent. It is a question of generating a new 'whole' by collapsing inwards the various parts in order to create a fresh, unique integrity. This is how the essence of action research has become a natural, organic and systematic part of school-based development. In the developing school (see Holly and Southworth, 1989) action research has become part of the way of life; evaluation (in the form of action research) has become **second nature** to development. No longer an after-thought, evaluation is built-in and planned for like development itself. Indeed, given the closeness of their relationship, it is becoming impossible to tell them apart. School-based action research is school-based development.

These observations are mainly — although not exclusively — based on some recent work in the Pacific Northwest of the USA. Over a period of three years I have been working as an action research consultant with teachers, their schools and their school districts, as part of the activities of the Puget Sound Educational Consortium (PSEC), Project LEARN (see Sagor, 1991), the Bellevue Evaluation Project and Washington State's Schools for the Twenty-first Century initiative. In addition, I am contracted to work on a similar basis with NEA's Learning Lab school districts and Mastery in Learning schools. My involvement in all these initiatives consists, typically, of working on two levels: leading training workshops and then making site-based consultancy visits. The workshops, as Sagor (1991) has argued, are crucial in gaining the engagement of the team-based participants. The workshop design involves participants in not only learning about action research by doing action research, but also focusing on their real needs (which are identified during the workshop process). It is at this point that the action research takes on a life of its own and ownership is transferred from workshop leader (henceforth, facilitator) to the workshop participants. One practical example will suffice.

In November 1990 an introductory workshop, led by Dick Sagor and I, took place in Bremerton, Washington State. One of the participants — a high school teacher (Toni) from North Mason School District, which is a four-school consortium involved in the Schools for the Twenty-first Century initiative — identified her focus area. She developed her interest in investigating why many of her students did not seem to be 'switched on' by their high school experience. As Shumsky (1958) said, this focus area was of 'deep personal significance' to her. She felt it was a real need which needed to be addressed in her school. So while the issue was significant to her personally, in her estimation it clearly had institutional significance. Between the workshop in November and a follow-up workshop at the end of January 1991, Toni collected her data by interviewing (both semiformally and informally) and surveying students in order to elicit their opinions, attitudes and feelings. She wanted to open up the affective domain in order to see what was happening 'on the other side of the mountain' (Drummond, 1986). She probably got more than she bargained for. When she turned up to the second workshop, Toni was in possession of rich and indepth data. She was in the process of analysing this data; but where next? Where could she go with the data? How could it be used to promote improvement; with the 'research' under her belt, how to move forward into the 'action'?

Simultaneously, and somewhat coincidentally, I was invited to work with the school improvement teams of the four North Mason schools (Toni's included). The issue was the same in all four cases: 'Having been in the 'Schools for the Twenty-first Century' initiative for over six months, why don't we feel that we're moving forward?' Frustration was in the air. Mobilisation was not happening. In the case of the high school, it was decided that a staff day would be organised at the end of February 1991 — with the purpose of unlocking and energising the school. The crucial decision followed: that the day would begin with a task session during which 'mixed' staff groups would be asked to analyse Toni's data (supplemented by similar data collected by a colleague on the school improvement team) and come up with 'issues', 'themes', and 'focus areas' in need of collective attention. This session exceded all expectations. It had three direct repercussions.

First, Toni's colleagues became hooked on what the data was

saying to them — it had become 'their' data and their issues; as one of her colleagues observed, 'It's no longer Toni's program, it's our program'. The transfer of ownership to the staff-at-large had begun. Moreover, and secondly, the data stiffened their resolve; it gave them cause for not only further reflection but also remedial action. Something had to be done, they said. Thirdly, the issues (common across all the groups when they reported out) gave them the focus areas (the bite-sized chunks) on which to concentrate. The task session concentrated their minds and their efforts. It provided the natural focus for their energies where none had existed before. Thanks to Toni, her colleague and their data, they — the staff — had found themselves and their real needs.

This particular 'case' has been discussed at some length because it illustrates not only how individual action research can feed into and become integrated with the process of institutional development but also how institutional growth — involving the thoughts and efforts of individual teachers, teacher teams and the whole staff — hinges on the identification of organic needs through the process of focusing.

It is of some relevance here that Sagor and Holly (1990) have identified six factors which, in combination, enhance the fortunes of action research in schools. It pays, they said:

- to have a *clear focus*, which provides clarity of both purpose and direction;
- to choose a focus which is *compelling* and has meaning for the participants — they have to want to work and invest in the area selected;
- to find a focus area with which enough teachers can identify in order to be able to launch into, and enjoy the benefits of, *collaborative inquiry*, ie. team-based action research;
- to embed the action research in a school's *culture of development* — the capacity and will to approach change as an integrated, systematic, coherent and organic process;
- to utilise both the advice and external perspective of *critical friends* — support agents who are attached (committed to and engaged with the school over time), yet detached in their observations;
- to integrate the action research in the *congruence*, consistency and chemistry of the Learning School, ie. the school as a learning system. It is not so much the action researching school, more a school that incorporates action research as a major component of its learning system.

What is clear is that points one to three above are about the importance of focusing, while points four to six are about **institutional development**. The following sections of this chapter represent an elaboration of these two major issues.

The need to focus

We have to deal with whatever prevents us from getting to the heart.

It's so important to be purposeful, not contrived.

People don't want this to drop, they just don't know how to take it up.

It's a case of giving them their wings to do it on their own.

Schools that aim to be self-developing often become self-defeating. In my recent experience I have found that schools attempting major change initiatives tend to be unfocused, fragmented, overloaded, confused, divided and incoherent. The teachers in these schools do not seem to know how to operationalise their visions and, as a consequence, they feel that their efforts are lacking purpose and direction; that they are not being productive; that they're not in gear and moving forward. This frustration adds to their stress levels. What are we going to do? When are we going to do something? These are typical questions. These teachers in these same schools tend to lack change processing skills. As a result, they seize on initiatives, take them 'off the shelf' and wonder why they don't 'take'. This haphazard, add-on/bolt-on approach to change means that 'they have programs, not a program' (Williams, 1991). They are not moving beyond innovation as faddism; there is no 'organised abandonment'; no understanding of Sizer's (1984) invocation that 'less is more'. Above all, their change efforts are not needs-related; they're artificial and contrived. It is a case of innovation and not development (see Holly and Southworth, 1989). The lack of self-discipline and process skills results in innovation overload — and more staff frustration (see Holly, 1991(b)). To make matters worse experimentation/piloting is confused with implementation, process is treated like content. Armed camps and factions from around innovations and institutional break-down beckons in a form of Balkanisation.

Yet, as some schools have discovered, the solution to this

particular bag of problems lies in their own hands. Focusing is a form of change therapy. It enables people to concentrate on the important tasks in hand (ie. to prioritise) and, as a result, to feel better — to feel an overwhelming sense of relief. Focusing gives teachers a purchase on change.

Finding a focus is one of the action research skills that has to be emphasised in the introductory training workshop. It is a skill (or set of skills) that is vital for teachers as action researchers and school developers to acquire. It is also a skill which has to be transferred to their colleagues back at school. While various techniques (including graphic representation and analytic discourse) are covered in the initial workshop, most reliance is placed on the technique of reflective interviewing. Participants are paired up (while remaining in their school/district teams) and are invited to interview each other concerning the preoccupations, interests, concerns, anxieties, doubts and hopes which pertain to them in their work situations. Above all, they are encouraged to explore the felt needs and priorities for development (both personal and institutional) of both participants. Their ideas are then fed back to the group (hopefully, in each case, the interviewer speaking for the interviewee); then, using the 'tambourine'* technique, individual and shared agendas are identified. When this process is repeated 'for real' back at school — in a full staff working session — the various groups will be asked to compare their tambourine-shaped notes/charts, thus leading to the identification of needs across the staff. The next stage is to invite volunteers to choose the themes/groups they would like to work on/with and, as a result, research and development teams are formed. 'Chunking' (see Peters and Waterman, 1982, and Goodchild and Holly, 1989) is what is happening here. Chunks (or focus areas) are identified and chunks (of the staff) form around them.

Both these aspects of chunking are mentioned by Peters and Waterman (1982). In describing their 'theory of chunks', they argue that it 'Simply means breaking things up to facilitate organizational fluidity and to encourage action' (p. 126).

It is a case of 'getting one's arms around almost any practical problem and knocking it off-now' (p. 126). Chunking, then, like action research itself, is about practical problem-solving and organisational fleetness-of-foot. It is, say Peters and Waterman, an important trait of an action orientation; it is about doing 'a string of practical tasks right', by making each problem manageable, doable and achievable. But these

---

* A Technique developed by Peter Holly for sharing ideas and developing a common agenda.

bite-sized chunks, emphasise Peters and Waterman, have to be worked on by temporary, interdisciplinary 'task force' teams, which, themselves, are the 'epitome of effective chunking'.

> The small group is the most visible of the chunking devices. Small groups are, quite simply, the basic organizational building blocks of excellent companies. Usually when we think of organizational building blocks, we focus on higher levels of agglomeration — departments, divisions, or strategic business units. Those are the ones that appear on the organization charts. But in our minds, the small group is critical to effective organizational functioning . . . Teams that consist of volunteers, are of limited duration and set their own goals are usually found to be much more productive than those with the obverse traits. (Peters and Waterman, 1982, pp. 126–27)

Above all, they argue, the true power of the small group lies in its flexibility — it provides a 'fluid, project-oriented environment'. The aim, then, is to build action-oriented flexibility into the system by building temporary, *ad hoc* teams of people who want to be there, who find the task themes compelling and who are willing to enter into research and development through the agency of collaborative inquiry.

It is important to point out that while techniques such as reflective interviewing sensitise staff members to the possibility of the identified issues being real needs (their genuineness has to be substantiated and confirmed/disconfirmed by further data collection), it is possible to operate the other way round, ie. to collect base-line data out of which flow the needs as diagnosed by the members of the organisation. In the case outlined above, however, both approaches came together. Toni took part in the reflective interviewing as a workshop participant and identified her interest/concern as student disaffection. She then gathered her corroborative evidence which was used by her staff colleagues for the purposes of both diagnosis and focusing their attention.

To sum up, then, focusing provides the following:

- the awareness and understanding of what really matters to teachers as individuals, team members and staff members — the school development program becomes grounded in their needs;
- the opportunity to promote issues arising from the teachers' everyday world — the classroom, the curriculum-in-action, the immediate context of teaching and learning. The relevance, practicality and down-to-earth quality of action research are

often remarked upon by teachers. As I have remarked elsewhere (Holly, 1990), 'action research is gloriously mundane';

- the appreciation of the need for a supportive data-base, which,
of course, is the stuff of action research;
- the wherewithal for chunking in the form of action research/
school development teams, the members of which share the
same 'span of investment' (Holly, 1990);
- the opportunity for these teams to embark upon collaborative
inquiry;
- the crucial process by means of which the personal, team and
institutional dimensions become linked and are rendered interdependent within and on behalf of school-based development.

Once the bite-sized chunks (or focus areas) have been identified, staff
energies and attention are channelled, targeted and aligned. Matrix
planning can be used to create a road-map — an integrated school
development plan, thus providing the framework/context for the
labours of the development teams. It is members of these teams —
clustered as they are around the focus chunks — who, on behalf of
their colleagues, now bear the brunt of school-based development.
Each team has to clarify its brief; maybe, even, redefine its task (what
do we need to attend to?). Each team has to create base-line data (where
are we now?). Each team has to establish targets, time-lines and success
criteria (where do we want to be?). And each team has to identify the
resource, support and training needs (how do we get there?). Their
planning may well have been accompanied by early trials/experiments
with their emerging ideas for improvement. Overall, they are readying
themselves and their colleagues for genuine, lasting implementation.
They are paving the way and increasing the likelihood of success for
real institutional development.

There is a need to recognise that the developing school has to be the learning school

School restructuring has to start in your own classroom.

It's not a spectator sport — we've got to make a difference.

Doing our school improvement plan brought us together.

It has been argued (Lewis and Munn, 1987) that action research can be
used for three purposes: understanding, monitoring and evaluation.

Figure 2.1   *Building blocks for school development*

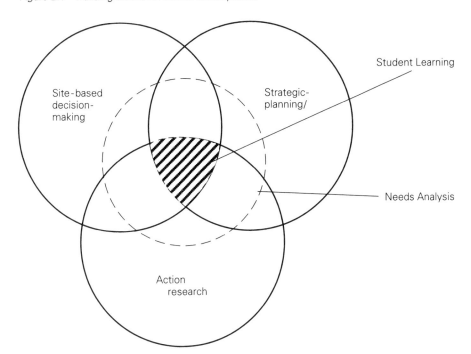

Indeed, action research for understanding (ie. diagnosis/needs identification) is the subject of the previous section. It is suggested, however, that mini-cycles — learning cycles — of action research can be used not only to fulfil the three purposes, but also to energise the entire cycle of school-based development. Action research for understanding, monitoring and evaluation provides the necessary depth and range of data required for informed decision-making throughout the cycle of development. But in order for it to play this vital role, action research has to become embedded and integrated within the various developmental processes. Moreover, as one building-block for school development, action research has to become crucially inter-locked with other building-blocks such as site-based decision-making and strategic planning; each then, gives meaning to the other 'partner' activities. Action research, for instance, *informs planning decisions* throughout the process of school development. This is another example of implosion and synergism. Each building block only achieves real impact and relevance when aligned with the other activities. Each cannot fulfil its true potential when standing alone; no one process is an end in itself. The 'end' is student learning and its improvement.

These building-blocks have to be integrated within a development culture (see Holly and Southworth, 1989) that promotes a climate of expectation concerning systematic growth. Thus, a level of intensity is produced which is cumulative, holistic and synergistic. But this can only happen — as Holly (1990) and Guskey (1990) have pointed out — if the integrative process itself has enough quality and impact in the first place. The power of school-based development lies in the quality of the 'mix'. What action research gives to the mix is the recognition that every school-based development has to be grounded in school-based research and, in turn, has to be researched for its effectiveness and impact. Between evaluation/research and development/action there is a constant, recurring dialogue. It is a conversation between equal partners, which are, ultimately two sides of the same process — like breathing out and breathing in. Mutuality and reciprocity help to create a process that is natural and organic.

The self-developing school is also the learning school. Learning comes from within and from the incorporation of critical friends and their external perspectives. Critical friends are 'critical' in three ways: they provide useful, constructive criticism; they raise essential issues by analysing the elements of the situation; and they are vital to the success and development of the learning school — they have the same impact as 'critical incidents'. Such support agents have to be external to the culture of the school and they have to have an anthropological intent (see Lightfoot, 1983). It is a case of generating supported self-evaluation in the form of joint reflection, which is essential for the health and growth of a learning system.

The learning school is the quintessential learning system. Its business is the enhancement of learning — student learning — and it is also a learning organisation. In the learning school, everyone learns. Moreover, as in all systems, a learning system has to be in balance; it has to be internally consistent. Holly (1990) has referred to the importance of systematic congruence. Within the learning/self-developing system, therefore, classroom development, school development and LEA/District development can all be aligned and underpinned by evaluation. Generic skills, techniques and processes like needs analysis/profiling/target-setting/individual learning plans (ILPs)/assessment, recording and reporting, may well have relevance for all those learning and developing in the learning school.

As Senge (1990) has argued recently, learning organisations are:

> Organisations where people continually expand their capacity
> to create the results they truly desire, where new and expansive

Figure 2.2   *Purposes of action research in a learning system*

PURPOSES \ SYSTEM LEVELS	Classroom	School	District
For Understanding	(To know where we are and what we need to improve)		
• needs analysis/assessment			
• data collection/analysis			
• action planning target setting			
• prioritizing			
• generation of success criteria			
For Monitoring	(To know whether our improvements are working)		
• formative feedback			
For Evaluation	(To know whether our improvements have worked)		
• application of success criteria			
• summative reporting			
• based on quantitative and qualitative data			

Source: Bellevue Public Schools, Washington State, USA

patterns of thinking are nurtured, where collective aspiration is set free, and where people are continually learning how to learn together.

Action research is the life-blood of the learning organisation. It provides both style and substance for the learning school. In such a school, teachers like Toni and her colleagues, learn together by sharing data and by learning from that data. Their collaborative learning then, has to be transformed into collaborative action. This is how the learning school (ie. the school as a learning organisation) becomes the developing school. Moreover, just as teachers enhance their capacity for collaboration by being collaborative, they enhance their capacity for collaborative inquiry by doing action research together. In so doing, their action research achieves the status of second nature. According to the dictionary definition, 'second nature' means a 'deeply ingrained habit' which is either 'long practised' or 'acquired so as to seem innate'. Combining these meanings, teachers, within their school-based efforts, are steadily acquiring the habit of action research by becoming well practised in doing action research. Returning to, but amending the words of the same song from *My Fair Lady* 'They've grown accustomed to its face'.

Throughout this present volume, the 6 'Cs' will reappear — indeed, they form the book's framework. The same can be said about action research itself. It reappears in various forms — as school-based review and development, as TVEI evaluation, as teacher appraisal, and the message is a consistent one: system change underpinned by a *spirit of inquiry* linked to a *culture of development*.

3   Achieving A Clear Focus: Whole School Planning

Isobel Roberts

It could be claimed that much of the educational change that has occurred over recent years has been externally generated, frequently by politicians or educational theorists, with teachers acting as change agents. Certainly little crucial change has been self-generated as part of a planned whole school approach that includes systematic monitoring and evaluation as an integral part of the process.

The result has been a series of *ad hoc* changes that schools have struggled valiantly to implement, frequently on the back of inadequate funding and often in a haze of misunderstanding or, sometimes, in a total vacuum. Through from ROSLA to the introduction and subsequent demise of language laboratories and on to the National Curriculum teachers have been required or encouraged to react to imposed change. This approach has done little to stimulate internally generated whole school planning that provides a coherent framework which is negotiated, agreed and understood by all. Indeed, it can be claimed that it has delayed the growth of whole school planning.

If one supports the notion of the self-developing school, (see Holly and Southworth, 1989) one must redress the dependency culture that the above system makes endemic by creating a climate in which open and collaborative debate can take place. One model, the CREATE approach (Figure 3.1) suggested by Holly, 1991, offers a useful framework for which a school can be empowered to take charge of its own growth and development. The institution is encouraged to:

- **C**onstruct a shared vision
- **R**eview current practice
- **E**stablish priorities
- **A**ction plan

Figure 3.1   The create model

- **T**ake the action
- **E**valuate the progress

Visioning is an effective method of not only climate setting but also uniting the staff as it sets out on the first stages of its developmental journey. By addressing a simple question such as, 'What sort of people do we want our pupils to be like when they walk out of this campus after six years with us?' the staff is focusing upon the total outcome of its collective professional life. Visioning addresses the whole issue of student learning and what the learning environment should be like in order to effect the desired outcome. It is an essential and effective goal setting exercise in which the school defines its *raison d'etre*. As Patterson *et al*. posit, quoted in Holly and Southworth 1989:

> In schools, clear and shared goals provide unity, help channel and target resources within the school programmes, can foster collaboration, and establish criteria for school success that permits assessment of progress . . . This takes the form of a clear vision of what the school should be, which is translated into concrete objectives and communicated to the staff in such a way as to influence what they do in their professional roles . . . Written school improvement plans can be a road map

for creating and realising a shared vision of what the school should be.

At the very centre of this discussion will be the distillation of the essence of what the learning process is about. It is the stage at which staff can examine their current practice as part of a retrospective exercise and in which they reassess their values and ideals in the light of their visioning and make revision as deemed necessary. It is also the stage where schools realise that they are actually doing much that could achieve their goal but frequently in a fragmented way. The necessity for a coherent structure to reflect the articulated vision is understood at this point. There is often a realisation that lack of coherence has resulted from too diverse a range of initiatives being tackled simultaneously. As Peters (1989) says in *Thriving on Chaos*, less is more. The need to do less well implies the need for the school to decide jointly on its priorities and focus its collective energies on ensuring that these priorities become the successful parts of the whole. Which brings the school to its action planning stage. Throughout the process the staff will have been involved in an on-going dialogue, either as a whole or in smaller interest-focused groups. All stages should be documented and made available to all staff so that the action taken is understood and agreed by all. This whole-school negotiation is more likely to ensure that staff understand why they may not be able to develop in a particular direction within the framework of this year's whole school plan, but will be able to do so as the process rolls on. This 'school on the move' (Holly, 1991), will make it easier to establish a system where all meetings and activities such as staff and departmental meetings, are part of the developmental cycle and lead into and out of each other. It helps to make obsolete the isolated non-contact teacher training days which have aroused antipathy amongst staff because they were frequently unfocused, disconnected and dislocated. The evaluation element is a fundamental and continuous thread that is woven through the process.

This CREATE strategy is by no means a deficit model. It highlights and celebrates the excellent and often unacknowledged practice that exists in almost all schools. In this sense it can be seen as an awareness-raising exercise that facilitates empowerment. Its central focus concerns itself with the notion of effective learning and on learning needs, which is what teachers understand as being central. Joint planning and shared responsibility make critical reflection both sharper and clearer. It is when they are required to implement *ad hoc* changes that they do not perceive as being concerned primarily with the quality of teaching and effective learning that they lose their sense of direction. By and large, teachers are tired of watching the educational kaleidoscope being vigorously shaken and waiting to see if the patterns that form will make some sense. This *modus operandi* has made teachers the victims of change: they are increasingly realising that whole school development planning places them in control of change. Hargreaves also argues for this in *Planning For School Development* (1989). In this document, he offers advice to governors, headteachers and teachers on how they can work in partnership to best implement the changes required by The Education Reform Act of 1988. He sees school development plans as a means of best managing development and change to make the school more effective: a method of enabling the school to 'organise what it is already doing and what it needs to do in a more purposeful and coherent way'. He also acknowledges that development planning can help to relieve the stress that teachers have felt as a result of the amount and pace of the changes they have been required to accommodate.

Whole school development planning was initially regarded by many teachers with suspicion, as another thing to add to the burden. Once engaged in the process most colleagues soon acknowledge that far from being part of the problem, it is the solution to their problems, a way of developing institutional competence. They no longer find it difficult to know which steer to chase, but are collectively engaged in keeping the herd heading westward. Participation in whole school development planning can reassure them that they are already members of a good school, but that they can jointly achieve a developing school that is also a thinking, learning and evaluative school. It encourages the creation of a developmental culture because it focuses on the way forward. It enables schools to articulate their internal agenda and better accommodate the external agenda within their own agreed framework. They can then internalise the external agenda as appropriate and proper within the avowed philosophy and good professional practice of the school: to improve the learning process. The developmental process is a dynamic one that needs to be managed. It is critical to the success of coherent whole school development that a key person is identified in each school to co-ordinate the development necessary to enable the process to take place effectively.

A professional development co-ordinator will need to ensure that all staff have access to the support that enables them to develop the skills necessary to improve the quality of learning in the classroom. It is essential that professional development co-ordinators receive ongoing training to support them in this critical role. Evidence suggests that in the self-managing school educational change is accomplished most effectively through the process of teacher development: thus it can be seen that curriculum development follows from teacher development, especially when that development is localised.

The scenario where advisory teachers work alongside teachers in the classroom has proved to be a most efficient and effective localisational model. The choice of this strategy for the implementation of *The Cockroft Report* (1982) was the first major move in this direction. Advisory teachers represent a clear articulation of the movement away from off-site courses and towards school-based teacher development. It is essential that proper professional development must directly involve and relate to the actual work and concerns of the teacher and not be distanced from that every day professional reality. Teacher development should ideally start from the teacher's own perspectives and environment and not from the political or theoretical context. Underpinning and supporting this in the self-developing school is the move towards personalised development where the individual teacher can choose a developmental menu to meet his/her own needs. Prior learning accreditation now means that work done by the teacher on behalf of the school can be rightly accredited as professional activity, within the framework of the more flexible award-bearing modular courses. The relationship with the teacher's own classroom reality is clearly enhanced through the use of strategies such as teachers as researchers and the keeping of journals. It is the remit of the self-managing school to help the teacher develop from his/her perspectives and context and also to encourage theory to be seen increasingly as the responsibility of the teacher as well as the provider/theoretician. The school needs to ensure that this individual development is integrated into and contributes to the whole school development initiative. In managing this dynamic developmental process, the professional development co-ordinator will also be on a learning journey. Learning and development is the growth aspect of a process that reflects the Eldorado principal '. . . to travel hopefully is a better thing than to arrive, and the true success is to labour' (Robert Louis Stephenson, *El Dorado*, 1879). We believe in a development culture that combines the best of the old with the best of the new, and that eschews mindless innovation. Within this culture the process, or the journey, is deemed to be as important as the outcomes or the arrival.

In most diagrams of development evaluation appears at the end, implying add-on status. The self-developing school needs to ensure that evaluation is integral to the developmental cycle and concerns itself with collaboration. (It should be about identifying strengths and

Isobel Roberts

building upon them). If successful, evaluation should disappear into the developmental cycle as opposed to appearing as a discreet aspect.

In a sense the form that the school's development plan appears in is an irrelevance. Initially, schools were encouraged via such documents as Hargreaves' (1989) to address the three questions: Where are we now? Where are we going? How will we know when we arrive? Many schools who have been involved in whole school planning are now sufficiently confident to turn these questions into statements that confirm: Where we are now; Where we are going; How we will know when we have arrived. They will necessarily have addressed the notion of success criteria in order to arrive at the latter statements. What is important is that the plan articulates the vision, the mission statement, collective philosophy and action plan of the whole staff, and also and very importantly, its supporting community. This will ensure the strength and purpose necessary to argue that the school is doing 'less well' according to its stated priorities, and that it will attend to the 'more' as appropriate according to its agreed plan. In the self-developing school the document will be available to all and will be presented to prospective candidates for posts within the school, to make them aware of the agreed philosophy principles and practice of the entire school community. The best documents also include long and short term plans with regard to the management and organisation not only of the curriculum, but also human and other resources as well as plant. Local Financial Management is the conduit through which the 'action planning' flows to become 'action taking' that articulates the school's vision.

This process of gaining greater focus to whole school planning can be seen in the way in which a county programme was set out for schools in 1988 and then in 1991. In 1988 the planning process was introduced following an evaluation of the County Inservice Education and Training (INSET) provision by Worcester College of Higher Education. It was sent out in a *Professional Development Handbook* with an introduction written by the Principal County Inspector.

INTRODUCTION

There goes more to it than bidding it be done.
                                    Royal Secretary to Charles I

The strategy for training and staff development in Hereford and Worcester will develop and change in the light of experience and the national context. A great deal has been learnt from the evaluation project commissioned by the LEA from Worcester College of Higher Education. As Francis Bacon wrote: 'crafty men contemn studies; simple men admire them; and wise men use them'. This evaluation report has been used to develop and refine an interactive model for training that will not only provide a programme of county activities but also encourage school focused activities to prepare and support teachers for the implementation of the national curriculum and assessment.

The clear aim of the training programme remains the development of activities that will improve the quality of teaching and learning in schools and colleges throughout the County.

It is important to note that there are two major thrusts to this strategy. First, school focused INSET, which is concerned with the needs of a particular school or college, will provide a planned development programme for every institution.

> A self-renewing school will be one . . . in which the staff regularly faces up to who they are, what they have and what they want, and, in figuring out how to get from here to there, will seriously consider paths they have never travelled as well as paths they know. J.I. Goodlad (1974)

Secondly, the programme of county activities will provide a programme focusing on a topic interest area or problem, which teachers from different schools have in common and on which they meet to share expertise and develop ideas.

It is vital that teachers learn to help themselves and to work with others to make the settings for their daily work better places for people to be engaged in teaching and learning. This handbook seeks to enable headteachers and senior staff to support positive staff developments in the interests of providing quality education for all pupils. It also seeks to explain in a straightforward way the administrative system and the procedures which should be followed when engaging in Local Education Authority Training Grant Scheme (LEATGS) related activities.

SCHOOL FOCUSED INSET

How to Prepare an Institutional Development Plan (IDP)

1   The Process
Headteacher in consultation with colleagues should:

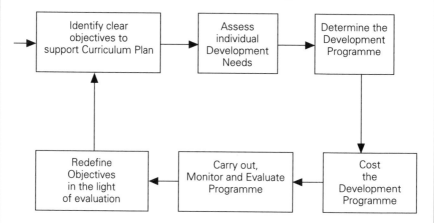

2   Preparing the Staff Development Plan
All schools should complete the proposal for inservice training support under the LEA training grants scheme. An indicative allocation of supply and funding will be sent out in the spring so that programmes can be drawn up by 1st June 1989.

In order to draw up the programme it is important that the needs of individual colleagues are identified. *One way to do this is to use a simple questionnaire. Examples of such questionnaires are given to help you to design your own development plan.* Hereford and Worcester, *Professional Development Handbook*, (1988)

In 1991 this initial approach had become more refined and increasingly owned by the schools because they had been involved in the production of a *Professional Development Co-ordinators' Handbook*.

THE INSTITUTIONAL DEVELOPMENT PLAN (IDP)

The IDP is the school's major planning process which brings together curriculum development and its supporting staff development. The process is recorded in the document known as the Institutional Development Plan.

The IDP reviews the ways in which the school has developed in the last year and establishes a broad plan for the future and specific targets for the forthcoming year.

There are three aspects of the document to consider:

(i)   the review of the past year (Where are we now)?
(ii) the plan for the future (Where are we going)?
(iii) the way review and planning processes are reconciled. (How are we going to get there?)

During the course of the year the Professional Development Co-ordinator will be involved in:

SPRING TERM

Review and Evaluation
The past year's programme needs to be evaluated under the following headings:

(i)   curriculum development plans;
(ii) staff development;
(iii) management issues, including pyramid and cluster initiatives.

Gathering Data
A wide range of information has to be gathered and assembled. Some ways of doing this include whole staff discussion, staff development committees, interviews, questionnaires, observation and document analysis.

(A range of examples used by some schools in this County are included at the end of this section. These can be adapted to suit your school if you wish to use them).

Setting targets
In deciding the areas of focus there will need to be awareness of national developments, LEA priorities, whole school and individual needs.

Consultation should take place formally through whatever

management structure the school has eg. subject area meetings, year group meetings, whole school meetings and with governors, and also informally. Staffing levels and finance will be natural constraints in this process.

From these discussions specific targets should emerge which may then need to be prioritised, agreed and communicated to the whole/staff.

The initial draft of the IDP is the end product of the Spring Term planning process.

This draft should be discussed by all interested parties.

SUMMER TERM
The final draft of the IDP should be prepared for presentation to the staff, governors and LEA and any other concerned bodies.

AUTUMN TERM
During the term the Professional Development Co-ordinator (PDC) should monitor new processes in operation eg. implementation of National Curriculum Statutory Orders and consider the effectiveness of data gathered during Spring Term.

The school will need to begin to consider priorities for the forthcoming IDP.

DECIDING HOW TO MONITOR PROGRESS AND TO JUDGE ACHIEVEMENTS

It is important to decide at the planning stage:

- how you will recognise the achievement of your aims?
- what evidence you will need to collect to enable you to do this?
- who will monitor the progress of the plan?
- who will collect the evidence of success?
- how and to whom it will be reported?
- how you will use the information you have gathered?

The following Figure 3.2 may help:

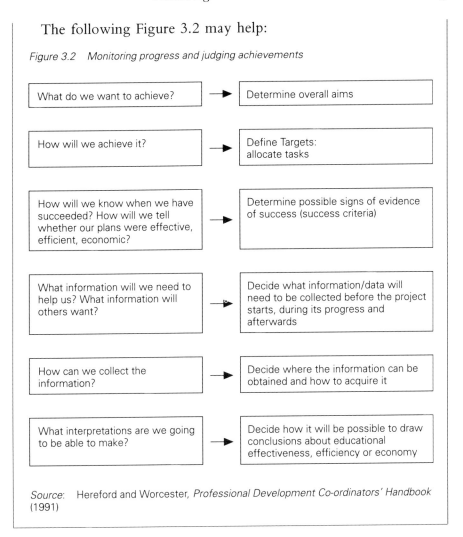

Figure 3.2   Monitoring progress and judging achievements

What do we want to achieve?	Determine overall aims
How will we achieve it?	Define Targets: allocate tasks
How will we know when we have succeeded? How will we tell whether our plans were effective, efficient, economic?	Determine possible signs of evidence of success (success criteria)
What information will we need to help us? What information will others want?	Decide what information/data will need to be collected before the project starts, during its progress and afterwards
How can we collect the information?	Decide where the information can be obtained and how to acquire it
What interpretations are we going to be able to make?	Decide how it will be possible to draw conclusions about educational effectiveness, efficiency or economy

Source: Hereford and Worcester, *Professional Development Co-ordinators' Handbook* (1991)

4   Creating a Compelling Agenda: Appraisal as a Co-ordinating Strategy

Jeff Jones

A recurring theme within this publication has been that of school and staff development. This chapter, with its emphasis on the appraisal of teacher performance, extends and reinforces this focus by advocating an approach which is founded on a professional development perspective. Appraisal and staff development form an integral part of the range of accountability measures now operating in schools. Together they represent a powerful initiative which can significantly improve the quality of education within our schools. This chapter looks at the purpose of appraisal, and its importance within the context of the school effectiveness movement, stressing that the central concern must be the personal and professional development of teachers.

For some years now, the Government has expressed the view, through a series of White Papers such as *Teaching Quality* (DES, 1983) that the teacher force continues to be the major single determinant of the quality of education in our schools. Few in the world of education would disagree with such a view. Having also declared one of its principal aims to be the raising of standards throughout the maintained sector of education, it is hardly surprising that the Government is placing such great store on the appraisal of teachers' performance as a means of securing quality control. Appraisal and staff development are certainly not new phenomena on the educational scene, but their emergence over the past three decades as agents of planned change is worthy of note. It is beyond the scope of this particular chapter to offer a detailed account of the origins of the appraisal movement. Figure 4.1 merely highlights the major influences on thinking in relation to the evolution of appraisal.

Among the reasons suggested for the national rise in emphasis and interest in appraisal are:

Figure 4.1   The main political factors influencing the evolution of appraisal

1961   Curriculum Study Group — set up to examine curriculum patterns in secondary schools
1974   Assessment of Performance Unit established by DES
1976   The Great Debate initiated by James Callaghan.

'. . . the educational system was out of touch with the fundamental need for Britain to survive economically in a highly competitive world through the efficiency of its industry and commerce'.

1976   The Auld Report — public enquiry into the William Tyndale School
1977   The Taylor Committee
1978   *Primary Education in England*, HMI
1979   *Aspects of Secondary Education*, HMI
1981   *Practical Curriculum*
1983   *Teaching Quality*, DES

'The Government welcome recent moves towards self-assessment by schools and teachers. But employers can manage their teacher force effectively only if they have accurate knowledge of each teacher's performance'.

1984   *Education Observed 3: Good Teachers*

'The one undisputed requirement of good education is good teaching, and performance in the classroom lies at the heart of the teacher's professional skill and of the standard of learning achieved.'

1985   *Quality in Schools: Evaluation and Appraisal*, HMI

'Staff appraisal involves qualitative judgements about performance and, although it may start as self-appraisal by the teacher, it will normally involve judgements by other persons responsible for that teacher's work . . .'

1985   *Better Schools*, DES

'. . . the regular and formal appraisal of the performance of all teachers is necessary if LEAs are to have reliable, comprehensive and up-to-date information necessary for the systematic and effective provision of professional support and development and the deployment of staff to best advantage . . .'

1985   *Those Having Torches* (The Graham Report)
1986   Education (No. 2) Act

'The Secretary of State may by regulations make provision for requiring LEAs . . . to secure that the performance of teachers . . . is regularly appraised.'

1986   Appraisal/Training Working Group (ACAS)
1987   Appraisal Pilot Study
1988   Education Reform Act
1989   *School Teacher Appraisal: A National Framework*

'Appraisal shall be an integral part of the management and support of teachers, and not an isolated exercise'

1989   *Developments in the Appraisal of Teachers*, HMI Report
1990   DES Paper issued to the IAC (December 1990)
1991   DES Draft Circular and Regulations (April 1991)
1991   DES Full Circular and Regulations (August 1991)

- A renewed sense of accountability at national and local levels, regarding the competence of practising professionals and the achievements of pupils. The rationale supporting this renewed sense of accountability is based on the belief that there is a direct relationship between teacher competence and pupil achievement and that teacher competence can be measured and be positively affected with appropriate training.
- A rapidly changing set of societal contexts and expectations are making new and increased demands on schools and teachers. This has been brought about by the legislation which has accompanied parental choice, the role of governors, the local management of schools, wider access of the results of assessment, etc.
- The stability of the teaching force as rolls of secondary schools continue to fall.

A major impetus for appraisal came from a somewhat unusual quarter, namely, the industrial dispute in the mid-80s. The Appraisal/ Training Working Group set up by ACAS during 1986 offered guidance on the principles and workings of an appraisal scheme, and further suggested that pilot schemes should be set up with these principles in mind. The working group saw appraisal:

> . . . not as a series of perfunctory events, but as a continuous and systematic process intended to help teachers with their professional development and career planning, and to help ensure that the inservice training and deployment of teachers matches the complementary needs of individual teachers and schools.

The representatives of the professional associations, the LEAs and the Department of Education and Science (DES) attempted to address this issue in 1987 with the establishment of the National Steering Group (NSG) for the schoolteacher appraisal project. The group's task was to oversee that development of the pilot scheme and to put forward recommendations for the establishment of an economic national framework for appraisal. The project, funded by the DES and based in six LEAs (Croydon, Cumbria, Newcastle, Salford, Somerset and Suffolk) offered the first significant indications of what kind of appraisal framework should be introduced. The experience of the pilot study was drawn upon by the NSG (1989) in making recommendations to the Secretary of State on the principles and processes which should underpin a national framework for appraisal. The NSG recommendations represented a potent vehicle for informed change, and has since formed a prominent footing for the recent regulations on appraisal issued by the DES.

The NSG principles were expressed as follows:

Appraisal schemes shall be designed to:
- (i)   help teachers to identify ways of enhancing their professional skills and performance;
- (ii) assist in planning the inservice training and professional development of teachers individually and collectively;
- (iii) help individual teachers, their headteachers governing bodies and local education authorities to see where a new or modified assignment would help the professional development of individual teachers and improve their career prospects;
- (iv) identify the potential of teachers for career development, with the aim of helping them, where possible, through appropriate inservice training;
- (v)   provide help to teachers having difficulties with their performance, through appropriate guidance, counselling and training;
- (vi) inform those responsible for providing references for teachers in relation to appointments;
- (vii) enhance the overall management of school.

The Secretaries of State have exercised the powers conferred on them via Sections 49 and 63 of the Education (no 2) Act 1986 to introduce the Education (School Teacher Appraisal) Regulations which came into force on 14 August 1991. A summary of the main requirements contained in the Regulations and the accompanying Circular appear in Figure 4.2.

The Education (no 2) Act 1986 establishes the parameters within which the education service is required to develop. Similarly, the 1991 Regulations and accompanying Circular set the framework for the development of appraisal. Significantly, however, neither can legislate for the relationships which make performance appraisal so vital. The appraisal of performance is crucial to all schools; unless the performance of teachers is managed successfully, no school will realise its promise. Other management aspects such as finance, resources, curriculum, pale into insignificance beside the effective management of teacher performance.

LEAs have clear responsibilities under the terms of the Regulation for introducing an appraisal scheme. Yet, there is a paucity of research

Figure 4.2   Components of the appraisal process

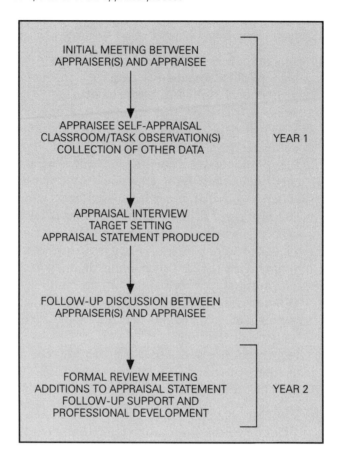

evidence on the role of LEAs in implementing change and innovation such as appraisal. That which does exist offers a series of broad guidelines. If an LEA is to introduce an appraisal scheme successfully then it should:

- take the school as the focus of change and the school culture as the ultimate target of policy;
- encourage the school head and staff to engage in a process of review prior to embarking on appraisal;
- provide resources, especially time and training, to support and nurture the process;
- maximize local responsibility for the innovation whilst recognising the responsibility of national bodies;
- provide leadership in the form of policy direction, and also plan for extension.

Figure 4.3   Example: LEA strategy for the implementation of appraisal

---

CONSULTATIVE GROUP
County Education Officer
Principal Inspector
Principal Officer
Inspectors
Professional Associations
Governors

- To establish the purpose and philosophy of the LEA's scheme
- To advise the CEO on the LEA policy
- To consider the recommendations of the Development Team and to agree the LEA policy statement
- To receive reports from the DES and to consider a local response to such reports

DEVELOPMENT TEAM
Principal Inspector
Inspectors
Headteachers
Teachers

- To plan the development of the introduction of the scheme
- To develop the LEA's policy statement on appraisal
- To recommend appropriate course of action on issues such as piloting, training etc.

The responsibilities referred to above include the establishment of:

- the overall management structure for the scheme;
- a framework for the scheme;
- the scheme's aims and objectives;
- local guidelines to support the scheme;
- criteria for classroom/task observation;
- regular consultation with professional associations and diocesan authorities;
- training courses for appraisers and appraisees;
- monitoring exercises so as to ensure consistency of arrangements within and between schools;
- monitoring structures to ensure that the outcomes of the scheme meet its stated aims and objectives;
- an evaluation framework in order to make improvements after experience and feedback.

As schools attempt to come to terms with a series of striking changes they will need to establish stronger links between school development plans, review, appraisal and inservice training. The changing pattern of school governance has, and will continue to provide schools with the added freedom to plan and act. It is ultimately only at the level of the school that planning, development, review, appraisal and training can be integrated and coordinated in a way which improves quality in developing schools. Getting to a stage where such activities are integrated will entail schools in varying degrees of adjustment.

The word appraisal can conjure up the feeling of threat within institutions. Indeed, performance appraisal has the ability to impose constraints and inhibit the development of an institution. However, used sensitively it also has the potential to set free and direct the creativity of teachers to the benefit of the children they teach.

The establishment of an effective appraisal scheme for the teaching force requires total commitment from all participants at whatever level. To facilitate the implementation of a formal system there is an initial requirement to establish acceptable guidelines, bearing in mind that associated with appraisal are often sensitive issues and far-reaching implications for the management of the school.

The climate in schools for the implementation of appraisal is crucially important and with something as sensitive as appraisal, the quality of management and the accompanying processes needs to be of the very highest order. Effective management is clearly required if any proposed scheme is to be accepted as a whole-school initiative and if any new procedures are to lead to greater effectiveness in relation to the major purpose of the school, which is to enhance the quality of learning.

Teacher appraisal, like any innovation within an organisation, poses challenges for managers. What may be different about appraisal as a new initiative is the added sensitivity with which it must be managed. Appraisal is likely to be seen not merely as one more initiative but, treated with the care and sensitivity it merits, THE initiative which will make it possible to harness the strengths of change in education.

The final approach adopted will depend upon a number of factors, not least the existing organisation and management style, along with external factors such as the LEA's policy in relation to appraisal and professional development. In general terms, however, the introduction of an effective system of teacher appraisal will rely on the extent to which the school has been successful in:

- building trust and understanding about the system through a genuine process of consultation with all participants in the scheme;

- presenting a clear and concise statement of the aims of the appraisal scheme and the means to be employed to achieve them;
- establishing a match between the design of the scheme and its stated outcomes;
- providing effective training in preparation for the scheme and subsequently during its formative stages.

The literature on appraisal has highlighted the following key principles which are considered to be supportive in the development and introduction of appraisal:

- there needs to be commitment and support from the LEA and the school for the process;
- the purpose of the scheme must be clearly defined and argued;
- the scheme must reflect the differing contexts in which teachers work;
- the process should be evolutionary;
- the system should be fully understood by all involved in it;
- all staff within the organisation should be appraised;
- job descriptions should be mutually agreed and updated;
- the process should start with self-appraisal; there should be a high degree of appraisee participation; and problems inhibiting performance should be discussed;
- observation of classroom processes should be a central part of the process;
- the appraisal discussion should concentrate on performance in defined areas and not on personality;
- there should be open, frank and immediate feedback to the appraisee;
- there should be mutually agreed targets for the forthcoming year followed by a review discussion;
- training in the skills of interviewing, observation, etc are required;
- formal appraisal should be an ongoing process.

The development of a successful appraisal scheme, whether at school or LEA level, requires a clear and coordinated strategy. The following staged approach is offered to the reader as a possible design.

Step 1 — Developing a Concept of Appraisal

For appraisal to succeed, it will have to be seen as an initiative which leads not only to higher standards of education for children, but also to the professional development and individual fulfilment of teachers. For this reason, the involvement of a wide range of staff in the planning of the appraisal scheme is crucial.

Developing a concept of appraisal is a crucial initial step in building a scheme. The development of a concept is an invitation to both the LEA and its schools to declare their particular slant or requirement for a scheme of appraisal. Appraisal in this way becomes context-specific since it interrogates the decision-making processes which relate to staff development and evaluation.

Prior to the articulation of a concept of appraisal, both the school and the LEA will need to debate a number of issues. Among them will be:

- the extent to which staff are aware of the background to appraisal, particularly in relation to the demands for greater public scrutiny;
- the range and nature of appraisal;
- the rationale for and the purposes of appraisal;
- the benefits and limitations of appraisal.

It is only after the discussion of issues such as these that staff will be in a position to develop a concept appraisal which responds to the needs of the LEA and the school in the current educational climate.

Step 2 — Developing a Framework for Appraisal

The successful implementation of an appraisal strategy requires the commitment of those for whom the scheme has been designed. This can only happen if staff are clear about the structure of the appraisal arrangements and the way in which it impinges upon their contribution to the school. Those with responsibility for managing at school and LEA level therefore have an obligation to make explicit a framework upon which their arrangements for appraisal are based. To facilitate the process of establishing a scheme of appraisal, guidelines must be laid down at an early stage. Such guidelines should stem from ongoing consultation with the staff involved. Issues which need to be addressed as the appraisal framework is developed include:

- generating ground rules based on the school's concept of appraisal — staff must be clear at the outset of the principles upon which the appraisal programme is to be based. The

procedures to be followed, the training requirements, and methods of gathering data and reporting should also be made explicit;
- contemplating the organisational issues and outlining strategies for dealing with them — organisations will need to consider what modifications need to be made to its organisation in order to facilitate the introduction of the appraisal arrangements;
- making decisions in relation to the precise format of the schemes — questions posed by staff will require considered responses:

> What will be appraised?
> Who will be my appraiser?
> Will I be an appraiser?
> How much time will it take?
> How often will the appraisal occur?
> How will the scheme be resourced?
> Will it be fair?
> Will findings be kept confidential?
> Will it be linked with pay?

- selecting the areas to be appraised — staff with a range of managerial duties;
- deciding upon the most effective and efficient methods for the collection of relevant data;
- deciding upon the format of the appraisal interview.

Stage 3 — Implementing the Appraisal Programme

Putting the appraisal scheme into action is an aspect of the general management of any developing organisation, and as such must be perceived as an integral part of existing management practice. Key considerations for management are:

- the creation of a conducive climate for appraisal;
- the selection of appraisers;
- the development of a timetable;
- the formulation of job descriptions;
- the training of appraisers and appraisees;
- the supporting of the process over time.

Stage 4 — Collecting Data

This stage of the process is based upon the principle that appraisal linked to professional development relies on the gathering of relevant data from a range of appropriate sources. This is a crucial element of the process if an objective view is to be gained of the performance of individual teachers. It will enable an appraiser to collect and analyse data from a broad spectrum of areas which help to make up the complex process of teaching and learning. Discussion at interview can be generated from this data and can encourage both the appraiser and the appraisee to consider ways of supporting professional development.

The selection of appropriate areas for data collection will clearly rely on the direction in which the school plans to move as well as the framework for appraisal determined by the school and its staff. However, typical areas include:

- curriculum review;
- classroom processes;
- pupil outcomes;
- wider school responsibilities;
- career aspirations.

Stage 5 — The Appraisal Interview

The appraisal interview or discussion provides a formal opportunity for the appraisee to discuss his or her performance with an appraiser. It is hoped that such an occasion will focus as much as possible on the central issues embodied in the process of teaching young people, as well as those items which may be of a more personal interest or concern.

The appraisal discussion is a two-way process which is primarily aimed at providing opportunities for:

- discussing performance in key areas;
- discussing career aspirations;
- setting professional development targets;
- re-negotiating job roles within the school.

In other words, the emphasis is heavily upon the professional development of the individual and subsequently the growth of the school in which he or she works. Much depends on the effectiveness of the interview and therefore a great deal of care needs to go into its preparation, delivery and the ensuing follow-up. Implied in much of what is said here is the need for skills to be acquired and developed through practice and sound inservice training.

Stage 6 — Post-Interview Follow-up

For the appraisal process to enjoy any degree of credibility, it will need to focus upon both the performance and professional development of teachers. As such, staff will need to be encouraged to perceive the interview discussion not as the summation of the process, but as the commencement of a cycle which establishes appropriate action plans and achievable professional targets.

Seeking agreement on the content of the final statement and setting the targets for action will therefore constitute a major aspect of the post-interview phase. It is evident that when recommendations for action have been made during the interview a follow-up procedure is called for. An appraisal process which gives rise to targets and strategies for improvement and development which may then not be acted upon, not only reduces the value of the exercise, but is likely to lead to resentment, demotivation and a waste of valuable resources.

Appraisal: A Coordinating Strategy

In a period of intense and rapid change, appraisal is urgently needed. Such a process is an entitlement. If teachers are to develop their skills and knowledge in significantly new directions then they should be offered the opportunity for systematically reviewing their work and contributions to the school. If appraisal is to have a place in the development of LEAs, schools and teachers, it will have to be embraced as an initiative which offers:

- greater confidence and improved morale for individual teachers;
- better professional relations and communication within schools;
- better planning and delivery of the curriculum;
- better informed references;
- positive feedback to teachers on their performance;
- opportunity for considering the job description;
- opportunity for negotiating the targets for the future;
- opportunity for discussing career development;

- constructive comments on the constraints the school may place on an individual's work.

Handled unfeelingly, appraisal can lead to frustration, self-justification and demotivation of teachers, resulting in a service which does not meet the needs of its clients.

Handled sensitively, performance appraisal has the potential to aid the development of teachers and schools. Moreover, it can provide a vehicle and structure which allows schools, areas, departments, as well as individuals within them, to respond effectively to current curriculum developments and other changes embodied in government legislation. Local authorities, schools and individual teachers are subject to a complex series of competing pressures, each worthy in itself but in need of coordination.

Appraisal cannot exist in a vacuum. Its long term impact on the performance and development of teachers depends on the extent to which it can coordinate and bring coherence to major legislative changes as well as other forms of review and development. The introduction of the national curriculum and assessment, together with the local management of schools represent current legislative changes. Initiatives such as the appraisal of headteachers and teachers, whole-school review, school development planning and inservice training are all related but must be brought together with skill and precision if they are to really influence school improvement.

The case has been made earlier in this book for the need for such initiatives to be supported by a thoroughly considered developmental plan. The introduction of appraisal, affecting as it does every single teacher within the school, offers a coordinating strategy — a binding force — for drawing together proposed changes.

There is, then, a critical interrelationship between appraisal and other important developments and reforms. The extent to which coherence is achievable depends on:

(a) the perceived functions of appraisal; is it to bring about individual and institutional improvement or to respond to the demands for greater public accountability?;

(b) the climate of opinion in existence within the organisation; this might well be gauged by the school's ability to manage a series of changes simultaneously.

It is inevitable that these contrasting forces are likely to give rise, not only to tensions but to opportunities:

(i) The process of whole-school review, as a significant element of the wider appraisal strategy, can result in greater management coherence in schools. This can lead to a more acute sense of direction and greater collaboration between fellow professionals both within and outside the school. A more coordinated approach at this level can lead to better informed decisions about resource allocation, budgetary control and staff deployment, for example.

(ii) A professional development model for appraisal, supported by imaginative staff development strategies, can provide a mechanism for ensuring a degree of accountability so favoured by politicians. The same cannot be said for an accountability model of appraisal.

(iii) In large measure, current reforms stem from central government — a top down model. Appraisal offers the teaching profession an opportunity of setting its own agenda for change by determining its own priorities — from below. This agenda will arise from self-review, an analysis of classroom practice, a discussion of professional strengths, and the setting of professional targets — each a significant element in the appraisal cycle.

(iv) Being a skill-based process, appraisal can support school development because it affects factors that are fundamental to how teachers and heads approach their work and how well they carry out their responsibilities for teaching and management.

(v) The distinct but inter-related components of staff development (policy, evaluation, planning and implementation), appraisal (data collection, discussion and follow-up) and school development planning (evaluation, audit, planning and action) offers much scope for managing the integration of all three.

(vi) Appraisal offers a strategy which enables schools to draw together their development plans, to establish priorities and to bring about a more 'bespoke' form of INSET.

(vii) The enhanced levels of communication which appraisal encourages between fellow professionals generates a more meaningful exchange of ideas and a sharing of sound practice.

(viii) At a time when schools are being held accountable for so many aspects of their work, the need for overt evidence that the school is taking very seriously its internal monitoring role is paramount. A well constructed appraisal scheme, approved by governors, which demonstrates not only that indifferent performance is being identified but that measures are being taken to improve such situations, will offer solid defence to those who call for greater accountability.

(ix)   As a major aspect of management and staff development, appraisal can do much to cohere and reinforce core and generic skills associated with training in these areas. Appraisal training should be integral to this coordinated training. In this way it is possible to avoid repetition, to reduce unnecessary pressure on schools and to maximise the use of available resources.

It is an indisputable fact that there are now statutory regulations in existence which cover the appraisal of teachers and headteachers in our schools. They are regulations which offer a framework within which schools can develop a scheme which suits them. There is little or no point in adopting a slavish adherence to a rigid schedule of appraisal. To do so would be to negate the major purpose of appraisal.

That there are, and there will continue to be major difficulties associated with the implementation of appraisal is undeniable. Nevertheless, it will be for the profession to maximise the clear benefits such a process offers, and minimise its shortcomings. With the education service placed so precariously at present, failure is not an option.

I end this chapter by quoting the words of T R Cornthwaite, Chief Education Officer for Suffolk: 'Giving time and attention to people pays high dividends . . . appraisal gives people priority'.

5 Undertaking Collaborative Inquiry: Evaluation for a Change: Inside a Development Programme

Denis Gleeson, David Turrell and Vincent Russel

Introduction

This chapter provides an account of the Hereford and Worcester Evaluation Programme (HWP), the principal aim of which is to both encourage modes of self-evaluation in school and to complement a cycle of review and development planning. Commencing in 1989, and ostensibly concerned with the evaluation of TVEI Extension developments, HWP has sought to fulfil two basic objectives. First to generate greater awareness and support for teachers engaged in evaluation and development work in their own institutions and, second, to give attention to how such work may inform the broader picture of action and development planning at school and LEA levels. Here, evaluation is not seen as something 'tacked on' to education development, but as integral to it, ie. as formatively informing the change process itself. In so doing the chapter charts the progress of HWP two years on in its development, and is divided into three main sections. The first, provides an overview of the thinking and rationale behind HWP and where school-based evaluation sits in relation to a growing centralism. Following on, the second section outlines in more detail the actual workings of the programme, in 'kick-starting' the self-evaluation process in schools. Finally, the third section deals with the way HWP has attempted to inter-link school-based evaluation within a cycle of development planning, review and school improvement, which complements other initiatives discussed in this collection.

Evaluation and Development

Innovation and change have been almost continuous features of the education scene in recent years. Following on the various crises which beset schooling and economy in the late 1970s and early 1980s, a wide range of curricular initiatives and reforms have emerged. Yet, if making schools more effective has been the battle cry of a decade or more of Conservative education reform, the quantitative and qualitative aspects of such reform are not easily reconciled. Although the Education Reform Act (ERA) (1988) significantly influenced the legal, administrative, financial and official base of schooling, this has not necessarily secured either the quality or effectiveness of educational provision in schools. More is needed, particularly at the level of understanding and responding to the change process itself. Terms such as the 'management and delivery of change' have an increasingly obsolete ring about them, conveying a functional and mechanistic view of change, largely divorced from practice. However, change is an elusive concept and even when celebrated is often difficult to find. According to Rudduck (1991) the challenge is to see the relationship between evaluation and change not as a technical problem to be overcome, but as a means of supporting educational development.

Yet ironically, the movement towards school-based development and evaluation coincides with an external climate of certainty which suggest that there are straightforward answers to straightforward questions. Increasingly, teachers and educationalists have come to see this question as problematic. If, at one level, the effect of legislation from National Training Initiative (NTI) (1981) to ERA (1988), has been to destabilise systematic educational development in favour of disparate initiatives, another way of looking at the present scenario of 'innovation without change' is to view such crises positively: to recognise what Blackman (1987) calls the spaces between contradictions '. . . which allow the possibility to legitimate and validate other alternative ideas'. Essentially, this is the climate in which schools have had to operate for more than a decade: at best working innovatively in and around the constraints of National Curriculum and Local Management of Schools (LMS) and, at worst, making progress out of crisis.

The implication here is that the imposition of central control, in the form of vocationalism, National Curriculum and LMS, is paradoxical and does not go unresisted. In Blackman's terms there are observable spaces, gaps and contradictions between the intended and unintended consequences of such policy, reflected in the simultaneous emergence of two potentially conflicting developments. On the one hand, it reflects strong central control of a kind which permits detailed intervention of government and employer influence right down to the classroom level (Harland, 1987). On the other, Youth Training Schemes (YTS), Technical Vocational Education Initiative (TVEI), LMS and school-based INSET, support local policy initiatives which in many cases, can be highly experimental and creative. If, perhaps, making progress out of crisis this way may not be ideal, it has, nevertheless, encouraged schools into new ways of thinking and responding to change, often driven by consumerism and market forces. Necessarily, schools and LEAs have been driven to be more evaluative, for a mixture of both educational and pragmatic reasons.

According to Hopkins (1988), the change in relationship between schools and LEAs, and the growing centralisation of Government policy, has led to new expectations that schools will play an increasingly more active role in monitoring and evaluation at local level. This is mainly explained by a decade of initiatives, associated with categorically funded projects and budget constraints, which has increasingly devolved curriculum development to school and consortia level, in pursuit of nationally agreed objectives. Such devolution has also taken place because the momentum of evaluation, monitoring, appraisal and quality assurance, cannot fully be handled at local level by Her Majesty's Inspectorate (HMI) and LEA alone. Moreover, changes in the governance of schools, LMS and assessment, including the statutory requirement that schools publish details of examination results, attendance and related matters, has made schools more sensitive about their image and more evaluation conscious. Thus, if the pragmatic process linking evaluation with development has arisen as much by default as by design, it has had a number of unintended consequences. First, in stimulating wider debate about the relevance and purpose of schooling and, second, in devising practical strategies for integrating evaluation and curriculum development, in ways which clarify the external/internal evaluation role. In seeking to inform such debate Holly and Hopkins (1988) discern three inter-related approaches to evaluation:

- evaluation *of* development undertaken by an external expert and usually involves an end of project summative report;
- evaluation *for* development: where external evaluator and internal developers collaborate to inform the formative process of development as it evolves; and
- evaluation *as* development: where evaluators are internal to the organisation and focus primarily on development, often with the support of an external evaluator or mentor.

Helpful as such constructs are it would be misleading to view them as mutually exclusive. If, evaluation *for* and *as* development are currently in vogue, it would be incorrect to assume that evaluation *of* necessarily represents an obsolete form of analysis. That would surely invalidate the important contribution made by independent and external forms of critical evaluation and research. For our purposes, the central issue is one of the relationship between external and internal approaches to evaluation, which involve a participative partnership (Fiddy and Stronach, 1987), combining both internal and external perspectives: '. . . what the external members have is "externality" from the culture of the school, and what the internal members have is knowledge of internal practice' (Hopkins, 1989). Thus, in seeking to achieve such a convergence Holly (1986) has argued for an emerging model of professional evaluation which is collaborative, formative, illuminative, non-hierarchical and where the evaluator acts as a 'critical friend'. The question is, what should such an emerging model look like, how might it be organised in practice and, perhaps more importantly, where to start?

Essentially, this is the question which has exercised the HWP team in planning the programme in the summer of 1989.[1] Though cognisant of various models advocating participative partnership, we found few working examples of such partnership to guide us, confirming Hopkins' (1989) observation that '. . . when I have seen the approach working it has been as a function of personality rather than infrastructure'. According to Hopkins, what is needed is a clearer indication of the conditions necessary to achieve the ideal of the emerging model, and the means to do it. In the context of HWP, this has been interpreted as: how to make HWP systematic in organising and supporting teacher, school and LEA involvement in a cycle of evaluation and development; how to create scope to allow teachers and institutions independence, initiative and flexibility in their formative responses to change and development; and how to communicate and involve all participants in decisions about data, evidence and dissemination in the programme. Consequently, the principal strategies adopted by HWP in realising such objectives, are discussed in the section which follows and which provides a more detailed account of the workings of the project itself.

Aims and Approaches of HWP

At the outset and from initial planning discussions with the LEA, heads and teachers in schools, it became clear that all parties wanted the evaluation to be *useful* (something of a message here), to *involve* participants actively and to *inform* education development in a coherent fashion. In current jargon it was envisaged that the main activities should be school or college based involving colleagues in self-evaluation procedures which encouraged analytical, rather than purely descriptive, accounts of 'What had happened?'. An additional requirement was that the model should be complementary to the developing structures of LEA and TVEI review systems including school and college development planning procedures. Through collaboration between schools, colleges, TVEI and LEA it was hoped to gain new insights into development processes and teaching and learning strategies. It was also intended that dissemination of outcomes might be helpful in informing the development and review processes identified in the development plans of establishments (Institutional Development Plan/TVEI review procedure).

In order to ensure long term growth it was decided to adopt an organic approach which involved running a number of relatively small scale projects which attempted to identify the issues and potential benefits of systematic evaluation. The support of senior management was enlisted where interest was shown and TVEI staff were to provide a supportive, rather than directive, role. The implementation model was therefore 'bottom-up', and 'top-down' where appropriate.

A number of pilot projects were initiated in the Wyre Forest Consortium with the objective of developing a practical framework for formative evaluation which did not impose a heavy workload on teachers and colleagues involved. The development officer responsible for evaluation in that area worked with colleagues in schools/colleges on a regular basis in order to provide guidance and to encourage a more formalised approach to self-evaluation. One of the outcomes of this work was the identification of the role of a 'local evaluator' which is referred to later in this chapter.

Evaluation activities were conducted by teachers in a number of establishments in the Wyre Forest Consortium. Involvement in the pilot was voluntary and decided as a result of negotiations between the development officer and interested colleagues. Initial contacts were made formally through correspondence and discussion in the consortium management groups as well as through informal channels involving advisory teachers and other TVEI staff who were already engaged in development work in some establishments. The initial projects took place between November 1990 and July 1991 and involved approximately forty teachers including ten senior management representatives. The nature of the projects varied considerably between establishments as did the number of colleagues involved in each establishment. Colleagues undertook a range of studies associated with TVEI themes, National Curriculum, active learning, cross-curricular and related issues.

TVEI staff and interested colleagues met on a number of occasions in order to discuss possible approaches to evaluation and areas of potential development. Having decided on the broad area for development participants were encouraged to focus on a more specific area for evaluation. Towards the end of the initial phase of HWP an evaluation seminar was held in order to review the outcomes of the pilot projects. The seminar was attended by the teachers and senior managers involved, and by representatives from the LEA/TVEI and higher education. Short reports were produced on each project which included examples of the following: developing teaching and learning styles in an English department; examination of the links between a high school and a special school; the introduction of information technology in a special school; some issues involved in job sharing; cross-curricular issues in delivering technology; and the work of a consortium working party (PSME).

The intended purpose of HWP is to support the development of the curriculum and/or teaching and learning approaches whilst providing evidence of degrees of progress. The basic philosophy of the model is that evaluation should be part and parcel of initiatives, whether large or small scale, and should be built in at all stages in the development process ie. throughout planning, implementation and review. Furthermore we argue that systematic and formalised evaluation acts as a spur to development whilst enhancing the professional judgement of teachers. INSET and school/college based support is designed to encourage colleagues to analyse the effects of any changes or decisions. Knowledge gained, as a result of analysis, then informs and influences future decisions.

Feedback from participants has indicated that the opportunity to undertake systematic evaluation supported the activities with which they were involved and encouraged analysis of their teaching styles and interactions with students. Information gathered during the initial stages of HWP suggests that the projects were formative and led to some staff development. A number of colleagues in Wyre Forest now form the basis of a county network of personnel and have been involved in subsequent phases of the evaluation programme. The following statements represent a cross section of views of participants involved in HWP during its first phase:

The involvement of students in projects varied but had generated an interest in evaluation amongst those involved. The question of the desired degree of student participation in self-evaluation was debated. Some students found self-evaluation and/or adjusting to flexible learning difficult. It was suggested that this was partly the result of a 'dependency culture' centred on the teacher. Strategies were needed to develop study skills, appropriate vocabulary for self-evaluation, and a supportive climate at all levels in the school/college as well as within the LEA.

There had been some opening-up of classrooms and greater sharing of experiences and expertise and evaluation had helped teachers to think about 'What was happening?' in the classroom.

The evaluation highlighted the need to adopt a team approach to planning, organisation, and teaching on courses such as CPVE. It also acted as a catalyst in bringing together staff leading to the identification of training needs eg. as whole staff training on IT.

Some teachers had identified the importance of 'process' as part of the curriculum and attempts had been made to understand the perspective of pupils as they experience a variety of teaching and learning situations.

The formalised evaluation report was useful in clarifying what had happened and in identifying problem areas and findings had been disseminated in some establishments. The evaluation had been formative and had led to 'action plans' in areas such as the curriculum, timetable, transport arrangements, and personnel issues.

Broader issues had been raised such as the reaction of management towards the projects and the role that it should play. In one instance the need to establish a timetabled course meeting had been highlighted and subsequently implemented. In some projects evidence was provided on which to base management decisions.

The presence of an external and 'neutral' evaluator was felt to be useful in a number of ways: a means of bringing more objectivity into self-evaluation; in helping to explain the supporting documentation; in bringing staff together; and in helping to disseminate findings. It was suggested that the evaluator could be 'on-call' in order to provide support at critical points of the evaluation.

Denis Gleeson, David Turrell and Vince Russel

Figure 5.1   How HWP is organised

Sixty-nine establishments including high schools, special schools and colleges of further education are arranged in six consortia

internal evaluators = teachers and senior management

local evaluators = TVEI curriculum development staff and advisory teachers who work with colleagues in schools and colleges

external evaluator = Professor Denis Gleeson (Keele University) working with teachers, senior management and TVEI staff

Recording of data was ongoing and a variety of techniques such as observation, field notes, photographs, etc, were used. Colleagues felt that they would be able to extend their repertoire of techniques in future evaluation work and that continuation strategies should be developed following an initial evaluation.

These initial experiences and outcomes were important influences on the development of HWP which, hopefully, is a more coherent and comprehensive programme geared to supporting school/college based self-evaluation.

The programme that has now been developed offers colleagues a practical approach to evaluation which takes into account the working practices and constraints of teaching and learning environments. The main elements of the programme include a minimum entitlement to:

- initial contact with TVEI evaluator in order to identify intended development;
- introductory and support documentation;
- participation in a residential programme;
- follow up sessions with the support from a local evaluator;
- a one-day evaluation seminar;
- completion of an evaluation report;
- dissemination within establishments and at LEA level.

All colleagues participating do so voluntarily following negotiations in establishments and within consortium management groups. In the early stages of the programme participants are asked to identify a teaching and learning development they wish to evaluate. In most instances the area chosen is too broad and some focusing is usually necessary before the exact nature of the project is decided. This process of clarification is useful in itself since it helps to ensure that primary, rather than secondary, problems are tackled and also helps to ensure that the focus of development is on teaching and learning. One of the purposes of the residential programme is to assist this process which, in some instances, may continue into the follow-up sessions.

The basic methodology proposed at this stage is illustrated in Figure 5.2 with colleagues being encouraged to look at situations from different perspectives including those of students, teachers, management, LEA, etc. There should also be some degree of group process operating in order to develop a common focus and a standardised view about what is trying to be achieved. It is also important for the role of local evaluator to be negotiated and clearly defined within the group. Summative reports are completed at an appropriate point which are usually interim, rather than final, documents and inform the next stage of development. Dissemination of reports within the LEA is intended to provide examples of teaching and learning developments and to assist others in the development of evaluation strategies. Documentation[2] and the role of local evaluator are designed to reinforce a formative approach.

The role of local evaluator developed in the early stages of HWP is flexible depending on the nature of the evaluation and/or the number of colleagues involved. The evaluator is concerned with assisting individual colleagues or groups to reflect on and to analyse aspects of their work. It is also a monitoring role providing time scales and clarifying evaluation procedures.

The residential programme, which has been developed as a result of feedback from participants, takes place over a two day period. A number of structured activities are designed to assist the identification of: prerequisites for development; planned stages of implementation; ways of building in formative feedback; management support needed; evaluation criteria; relevance to the school/college development plan; follow-up required. The residential course provides an opportunity for colleagues to spend blocks of time planning and working on their developments without the distractions that may exist 'in school or college'. As the residential course progresses colleagues are directed towards the evaluation issues and the relationship between evaluation and development.

Throughout the programme attempts are made to identify the management issues involved at a number of levels eg. classroom, department, establishment, etc. Members of senior management are encouraged to participate in order to provide sufficient support and

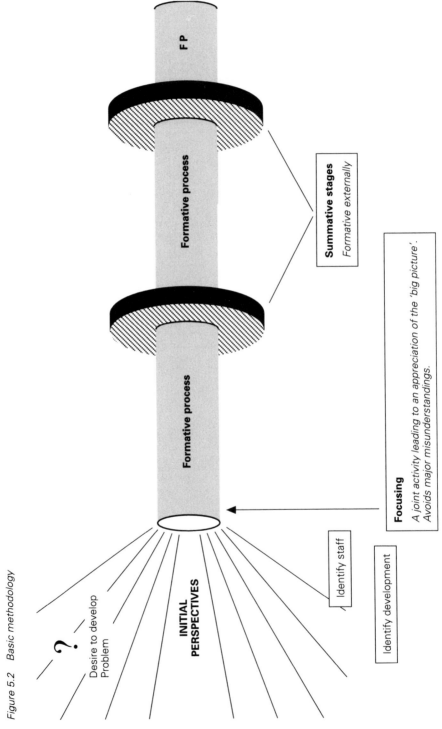

Figure 5.2   Basic methodology

status for the development. An additional aim of the programme is to develop continuation strategies for further evaluation work through adaptation and application of the evaluation model. The duration of the programme is flexible but normally lasts from six to nine months.

A one day review seminar takes place towards the end of the programme the purpose of which is to review progress in each of the projects. It is also an opportunity to exchange experiences and discuss problems that have occurred. During the seminar feedback takes place through groups who address a number of key questions which aim to highlight the evaluation issues and the development issues. There is also an opportunity to consider future steps that colleagues might take in order to disseminate their evaluation work. During the final part of the review day participants contstruct an action plan which clarifies the dissemination strategies they intend to employ.

Short reports (1500–2000 words) outline the major issues and findings of each project in terms of the management of teaching and learning. They also highlight enabling factors as well as problem areas. Reports may also make recommendations which are designed to ensure that development continues and are therefore summative in terms of the particular stage of development but formative in the longer term. They may be used to assist the dissemination process both within and between establishments but remain under the control of individual establishments. Reports are one element in the dissemination process which also occurs through a network of participants and via the INSET programme.

To date eight programmes have been run and more are planned for the academic year 1993–94. A recent innovation has been the development of a programme for senior management.

Additional support for colleagues involved in HWP has been provided through a series of workshops run by the Centre for Social Research in Education (CSRE) at Keele University namely the 'Teachers as Researchers' programme. The workshops were led by leading practitioners and served to illustrate the scope of evaluation models and practices in a number of LEAs. The link between TVEI and Keele has been an important and developing feature of the programme with colleagues from Keele being actively involved in the residential programme, report writing and the development of documentation. Regular contact with institutions of higher education has, by providing an external perspective, helped to prevent the developing model from becoming too narrowly focused and parochial. Formal and informal links between TVEI and the LEA have been established and a county co-ordinating group, which includes representatives from higher education, oversees the development and implementation of strategies many of which are reflected in this collection.

Some Observations on the Model

Initial reactions of participants involved in HWP suggest that evaluation is a worthwhile process but that 'there is not enough time to do it', or that, 'we do it already'. There is, of course, some truth in these statements but early signs are that the model developed addresses these comments in terms of providing a more systematic approach to evaluation. In our view the provision of a relatively unobtrusive framework, which can be adapted to fit into existing organisational arrangements, is as important as providing time. The monitoring and support role of local evaluator has proved to be a way of capturing the evaluation that, undoubtedly, does occur throughout much a of teachers work.

There is, however, a 'squirm' factor operating in some instances which may occur as a result of suspicion about the motives of those promoting evaluation activities and/or preconceptions and worries about 'What?' or 'Who?' is being evaluated and 'For Whom?': essentially the audience question. Colleagues need to be reassured that the focus is on all the issues concerned with a particular 'development' rather than individual teaching performance. Reservations have tended to disappear once those involved have defined the specific parameters of the evaluation, a process which also simplifies the evaluation process. Moreover, TVEI staff have observed a growth of confidence amongst some colleagues, particularly those who have involved students and/or engaged in peer observation, in terms of their willingness and ability to undertake further self-evaluation work.

Encouraging participants to look at evaluation and development as one process has, in some cases, caused initial difficulty as a result of perceptions held that 'evaluation is done at the end after the implementation stage'. The residential programme has helped in this respect by providing an environment where 'problems can be thought through' at the beginning. Another area of difficulty, is in the identification of success criteria which most colleagues find difficult particularly when attempting to achieve a balance of quantitative, qualitative, cognitive and affective criteria eg. in areas such as equal opportunities, PSE and so forth. However, having identified criteria, this part of the programme is arguably the most useful to participants since it provides some yardsticks against which to start thinking about how to 'measure' development.

An important and interesting aspect of the programme has been the developing role of the 'local evaluator' which is key to the development of dialogue and trust between colleagues in establishments and TVEI staff. The presence of a local evaluator in group situations often helps participants to focus on the evaluation issues as well as the issues of development. At certain stages of the programme, for example when attempting to identify what those issues are, the evaluator can be a catalyst in stimulating debate. Being external to the establishment the evaluator is neutral and thus free from internal political influences. In this situation the evaluator can act as a sounding board for ideas and concerns which can be discussed in an objective and positive manner. This form of collaboration ensures that guidance and monitoring takes place through regular meetings. There are also other benefits since the involvement of 'external' personnel adds weight to the evaluation and enhances objectivity since an external perspective is provided. Staffing could be a problem in the future as the programme expands. In-service training has, however, been undertaken by a number of curriculum development officers and advisory teachers who are increasingly becoming involved. The purpose of the training, and parts of the residential, is to make explicit the supportive role played by a local evaluator. Mutual understanding of this role by participants and evaluators makes the follow-up work easier. In essence a 'partnership' model has been developed.

The involvement of senior management in some projects has helped in two main ways. Firstly, by providing support and status for teaching staff involved, the implementation has proceeded more quickly. Secondly interested senior managers have been able to apply the 'helicopter factor' ie. to take an overview of what is happening, not only in terms of the development, but also in terms of the evaluation processes occurring. In several instances, following an initial project, further work has been carried out within the establishments involved where the evaluation model has been applied in other curriculum areas. Additional programmes are now being planned which are designed to support members of senior management who are engaged in the development of whole school approaches towards evaluation.

In projects where the degree of support from other colleagues is high teaching and learning developments have proceeded more quickly, particularly if senior management are involved and/or recognise the potential value of systematic supported self-evaluation. This conclusion has been reached as a result of observations of group activity during the residential courses and subsequent initiatives and implementation in members' own establishments.

The residential course and a one day review seminar offer opportunities for colleagues to come into contact with a variety of other initiatives. Discussion of projects helps participants to clarify their thoughts about their own projects whilst broadening knowledge and experience of the work of others. One of the most encouraging aspects of the programme is that as the follow-up work in establishments gets underway any initial scepticism recedes while enthusiasm tends to endure. To most participants the value of a systematic approach to evaluation becomes apparent during the programme. This development is put to good use in subsequent programmes when some of the 'past participants' attend the residential in order to give a 'warts and all' view of their experiences.

One of the strengths of the programme has been the extent of collaboration between teachers, TVEI personnel and representatives from higher education. Classroom practitioners involved in teaching and learning developments have received local support from TVEI and, as a result of involvement of colleagues from Keele, have also developed an awareness of broader evaluation issues and some knowledge of initiatives being conducted in other LEAs. The link with Keele has ensured that a broader range of perspectives and expertise have guided the development and implementation of the programme. The task of TVEI staff has thus been to develop a programme which is systematic but also practical and workable within the constraints under which teachers operate. In general this collaborative model has helped to avoid a parochial approach to evaluation and has resulted in more openness, sharing of concerns and greater objectivity as a result of appreciation of a wider range of perspectives.

The degree of student involvement in some projects has been significant and in these cases the quality and depth of evaluation has been enhanced. Recent programmes have emphasised the importance of student participation and have suggested strategies for their involvement. A number of teachers have been very creative in the ways in which they have involved students adopting a number of approaches to gathering data ranging from the use of video and audio-visual techniques to individual and group tutorials.

The HWP model has developed collaboratively but has been consistent in its aim of maintaining a clear focus on the development of teaching and learning styles in the classroom and the appropriateness of these to the needs of students. The model has also been developed within the context of the growth of development planning and review at LEA, TVEI and school level. Unfortunately the decline in the role played by TVEI and the uncertainties facing LEAs cast shadows over the future of HWP and its role in school development and change. Strategies need to be developed soon if HWP is to play a part in maintaining progress towards an evaluation culture and further development of teaching and learning approaches particularly in terms of the effects of LMS and National Curriculum in limiting new thoughts about curriculum innovation and change. Managing curriculum and costs is one thing: ensuring education development is another. It is to this aspect of the debate that our attention now turns.

HWP in Relation to Planning and Identifying Change

The actual process by which change and development in projects such as HWP takes place can be more mysterious to the participants than is generally acknowledged. This is because it is essentially a human activity which relies on the constant redefining of the perceptions of those involved. This is not to ignore the substantial professionalism and efforts to plan coherent and systematic structures for growth and development. However, development that recognises the contribution that participants will bring to this organic activity cannot prejudge either the outcomes or the final form it will take. Indeed in beginning this work we anticipated a diversity of response. We wished ownership to be with the participants, we knew that this would mean that they would shape and mould the developments as they became their own. Although this organisationally is more difficult it was essential if we were to adhere to our key principles.

The model described in the previous sections outlines the principal aims and mechanisms of the programme. Clearly, the main purpose of the programme is to support colleagues involved in the development of teaching and learning approaches. A consequence of the programme and the way it is constructed is the wider application of self-evaluation procedures and the generation of tangible evidence recorded during the evaluation and in the form of a summative report. Dissemination takes place in the following ways: informally and formally within departments and establishments; through the local evaluator contact with other establishments; via the review seminars where colleagues share experiences; and through the distribution of summative reports or other documents. The findings and conclusions of teachers involved are highly relevant to, and can inform, planning and review procedures at establishment or LEA levels. The model, therefore, offers a method of linking the core activities of teaching and learning with review and planning.

Figure 5.3 summarises the main approaches to evaluation adopted by the LEA and TVEI. A variety of approaches have been adopted and may be cross-sectional, longitudinal or integrated. The diagram attempts to show the relationships of the Formative Evaluation Programme to other procedures and initiatives. The top of the inverted pyramid indicates that the programme is concerned with the core activities of teaching and learning where evaluation may be regarded in terms of *for* or *as* development. In general activities take place at a micro level being concerned with small groups of individuals or departments. One aspect of the programme is that it provides raw material or data which can influence planning and review. In this respect it forms part of the TVEI review structure and can do likewise for the LEA. In addition findings might be more relevant to more macro activities concerned with accountability.

TVEI procedures involve the central team in the construction and publication of an annual plan or 'Framework for Development' which highlights the priorities for the year and sets out in detail target areas for curriculum development, planned stages for development, success criteria and expected curriculum outcomes. These provide a backcloth against which consortia and establishments can plan with formative evaluation providing a means of implementing change and assessing the extent of the development.

The possibilities of HWP are that it provides a framework within which development can be planned, implemented, monitored and evaluated. The programme has acted as a catalyst, encouraging teachers to reflect on the effectiveness of their teaching methods and to share their work and experiences. Many teachers have been motivated by the interest shown in their work by 'outsiders'. The external/local evaluator role has in several instances facilitated group process and group development whilst maintaining the focus of activity on the core educational issues. The completion of a short report can clarify the key issues involved in a problem or development and can also go some way towards addressing accountability issues. An added advantage to participants is that the model is flexible and can be adapted for use in a range of different situations.

The main limitations of the programme are concerned with time and resources, suspicion or anxiety, and continuation of evaluation following an initial project. The amount of time 'out of the classroom' has been minimised but is still a cause for concern in some cases. Where possible administrative structures such as faculty or departmental meetings should be used in order to minimise the need for 'additional' meetings. This is particularly successful when evaluation is given

Figure 5.3   Summary of evaluation strategies

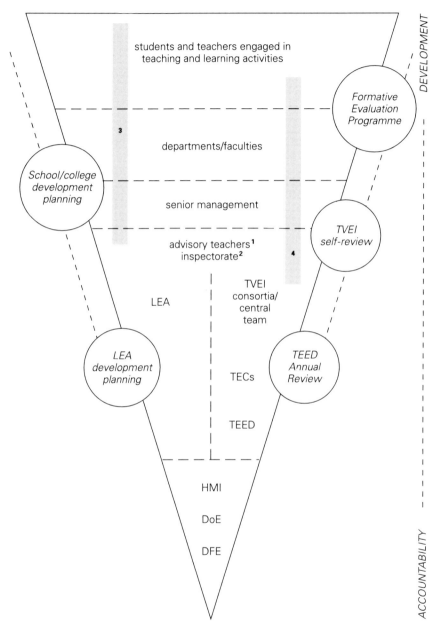

1   Worcester College of Higher Education
2   Keele University
3   Successful Schools Project — Keele University
4   Other projects e.g. Action Planning; Extension Database; E-mail; etc

a regular slot. The way in which approaches to evaluation are introduced is important and emphasis should be given to the supportive and empowering aspects of formative evaluation in order to overcome perceived threats. A key question is 'What happens after an evaluation?'. Unless senior management become involved there is no guarantee of a continuation of systematic evaluation. A whole school, or consortium, approach to evaluation may be needed to ensure a coherent and consistent approach.

On balance it is our view, and the view of many participating colleagues, that the net benefits of HWP are substantial both in terms of increasing professionalism and developing understanding educational processes. It is important, however, that continuation issues are addressed and further work needs to be done on finding ways of integrating formative evaluation with existing structures in establishments in order to support the development process. It is important, however, that TVEI and the LEA continue to promote an appropriate 'climate' which supports and nourishes the 'green shoots' which are now in evidence.

Organic growth does not mean that there should not be basic principles on which to organise future support nor does it mean that there should not be a structured, rational, coherent and systematic form of development. A prerequisite for organic growth in education must be the provision of a conceptual framework to which professional colleagues can sign up. It is essential that we share or at least accept common principles on which to base our professional action and interpret these principles using an agreed conceptual framework. The framework becomes the basis for climate setting in schools and LEAs. HWP was faced with three emerging questions:

- What are these basic principles?
- What is the conceptual framework?
- What actions and activities need to be planned, in what sequence, in order to ensure development becomes part of the professional life of the participants?

To say that HWP had anticipated all avenues of development would negate the principles of self-managing, self-developing, self-reviewing establishments. However two principles are clear. Schools and colleges would only grow healthy and become more effective if they were empowered and if they empowered colleagues within their organisation. Secondly, that establishments and LEA's should be 'communities of learners' and therefore the processes by which people learn are common for students, staff and the LEA. These principles accept that education is a life long activity and some of the needs of learners are common. It is the context in which they act out their learning which differs. Increasingly, the introduction of a range of flexible approaches to learning in schools and colleges heightens the commonality of learning processes.

It is and has been a major task of TVEI and the LEA to translate into action the development of these two principles. It is in order to see these principles in action that it is essential that colleagues in establishments and the LEA share a basic conceptual framework. This framework will assist in determining their future actions and is embodied in the cycle of the LEA's planning, TVEI planning, Institutional Development planning and the planning for effective classroom management. The acceptance of this framework therefore needs to operate at many levels: at LEA level, at consortium level, at school/college based level, at departmental level and by individual teachers expressing professional judgement in their classroom management. It is this acceptance of the fundamental conceptual framework which gives teachers, senior management and the LEA officers the common 'tool kit' for planning. The challenge is how to assist in setting the climate in order to ensure that the conceptual framework is generally accepted, and then embodied in the everyday practices. Across a large LEA uniformity should not be expected, even if it were desirable, but there are increasing signs of common planning approaches.

In an LEA where TVEI Extension is based upon a high degree of development three sites for curriculum and in-service planning and development emerged. The school's or college's own development plan, the consortium planning meetings and central LEA and TVEI. It is important that good and clear communication exists between each of these groups of people as they set their own targets. It is essential that each should have a clear view of the intentions of each other. The three levels of target setting, using the same process, the same conceptual framework, must be carried out as an interlinked activity, each constantly informing the other. This creates greater opportunity for collaborative activity. It has been the perception of colleagues that these opportunities assist in a more coherent form of development, supporting their professional growth and their ability to manage the substantial changes in which they are involved.

The fundamental contribution that TVEI Extension has made to this process is to assist in gaining acceptance of the value of this conceptual framework at all three levels and to look for ways to systematically support establishments in taking a more holistic approach to planning. This was encouraged by ensuring TVEI targets corresponded with the development and delivery of the National Curriculum through a process of self management. As in much development many key areas are fragmented. It was the concern of TVEI to forge these fragmented elements into a more coherent whole. To be able to do this requires new perspectives to be sought. Achieving a new perspective is an interesting process in itself not dissimilar from taking an object and blinking to try to make it change shape in front of your eyes. Both can cause nausea. However, seeing fragmented development from a different perspective helps in producing new connections. TVEI was urging that planning processes and learning processes had much in common for all of the community of learners. These links can help to forge a coherence. It was by looking for a holistic process to development, looking for the links, and by recognising common features in the process of learning for students, staff and officers that it was possible to identify common management strategies, skills, structures and actions.

It may be useful at this point to consider what common elements can be interlinked. In HWP it became apparent that more clearly defined approaches to the management of learning were necessary — this need was articulated by colleagues themselves. There were, however, different contexts: senior management; middle management; and classroom management. In these contexts there were common or generic skills, ie. target setting, reviewing, negotiating, listening, decision making, communication, etc. The development of these skills had, for many colleagues, historically been left to chance and, therefore, there was a need for a systematic approach to their development. It was clear, of course, that the context was highly significant. The classroom teachers needed these skills to be based around the development of the management of learning in subject areas of the National Curriculum, middle managers around team building skills and senior managers in leadership activities, but it was their commonality which assisted in the important activity of establishment climate setting. A climate which recognises all participants as learners, all needing their own critical friend, all needing to take a greater responsibility for their own learning and all understanding that they are accountable for their own actions. A climate based upon trust and mutual support, rather than on hierarchy and control. The contradiction between this and what was happening at national level was not lost on many participating. HWP is assisting in this more holistic developmental approach by offering a range of in-service development for colleagues with different responsibilities, classroom teacher, head of department, senior management but, drawing attention to the necessity of the enhancement of common skills and the inter-related nature of the planning processes.

The methods for addressing these different contexts were varied. Consortium based programmes were organised in Effective Leadership for senior managers which looked at a simple structure based upon Action Centred Leadership. This recognised the relationship between Task, Team, and Individuals. Programmes of INSET were organised by consortium and TVEI Central Team for developing individual skills of listening, negotiation, and reviewing. Very substantial work was being done developing strategies for the management of learning. These different levels reinforced each other in their common approach to a community of learners. As the conceptual framework being used at all levels is based upon a commonality of process, ie. planning, organising, providing, maintaining, monitoring, evaluating, (Brighouse, 1991) each activity organised through TVEI was mutually supportive, a factor which contributed to overall climate setting.

It was fundamental to this approach of holistic management that the core of all activity should be the development of more effective teaching and learning. The need to see the links between a whole school approach to learning experiences, guidance systems based upon action planning, records of achievement, equalising opportunity, the growth of individuals and achievement in its broadest sense became critical. Formative evaluation working at each level of an establishment became the means by which the cycle of planning could be closed. Common principles, a common approach and common skills assisted in drawing together what was frequently a contradictory and fragmented set of activities. We are, however, only two years into these processes of development, the relationships between the players are numerous. We will expect the form of the developments to change further as the level of our awareness is raised collectively.

The emphasis of the evaluation process was not perceived by the main participants (LEA, TVEI, schools and Keele University) in the same way. This difference in perception became the catalyst for interesting discussion and subsequent development, an open self-critical air prevailed and a realisation that it was possible to build a practical approach to holistic management and development. There were no other examples of this systematic approach readily available in other LEAs. The mix of ingredients were unique and this allowed for new perspectives. However, these developments had to operate within other frameworks. There was a fundamental issue of accountability, the funding for TVEI came from the Department of Employment, they had their targets, and the LEA was accountable for the use of this substantial external funding. It was a requirement to develop a system of review to service this accountability. Through discussion with the LEA Inspectorate, the TVEI Central Team, TEED, the consortia and the schools and colleges it was agreed that the review system would be based upon a system of target setting and development, and a system of evaluation based upon both qualitative and quantitative success criteria grounded in the developmental activity of the schools and colleges. In addition, it would link to a system of reviewing by TVEI Curriculum Development Officers, County Inspectors and TEED Education Advisors but, significantly the ownership is with the establishments and is based upon a system of self-evaluation. This ensured the integrity of our key principles that development which includes evaluation is a systematic process which is fundamentally school or college based, but is influenced and moulded through a variety of external forces.

Conclusion

This chapter has sought to give an insight into how one TVEI Extension programme has sought to embed TVEI targets into the National Curriculum. In attempting to do this TVEI has been able to gain support from and give support to an LEA and its schools and colleges as they undergo substantial change: change which nationally is not clearly defined. In order to ensure that we don't lose sight of the fundamental issues in the maelstrom of change it has been the policy of TVEI to focus on what happens inside educational experience. TVEI targets are supporting these experiences. To achieve this it was plain that we needed to raise teacher expectations of what is possible and to support colleagues on all levels in developing attitudes and values which put children and young people at the heart of the educational experience. It became clear that it was important to support colleagues as they changed the culture of their establishment. It was necessary to help generate a common vision, a vision which does not divide off the learner from the teacher (although recognises their different needs), a vision that states that all people continue to learn and a vision which looks for practical ways to provide more appropriate ways for this learning to take place. Formative evaluation as an integral part of development is not just a useful mechanism but a philosophy which puts process on an equal footing with knowledge and skill. It is our belief that management models which do not embrace a whole school approach, departmental structures that do not look outward as well as inward, pastoral structures which are divided off from learning processes, and single methods of learning represent and belong to 'schooling' of a different time. These will be unhelpful to our nation and our young people in the next millennium. What is needed is a common conceptual framework which provides for clear systematic planning and development but is based on a commonality of purpose for all participants. This commonality should not be confused with a uniformity: it is an acceptance that we all have a responsibility to plan, to provide, to review, to communicate, to listen, to support and to collaborate which is important in the climate change. Formative evaluation has as a prerequisite openness, confidence in professionalism, and a willingness to share. Essentially it is seen to enhance professional judgement at a time when many teachers feel professionally de-skilled.

In an ERA of competitiveness with LMS, Grant Maintained Schools (GMS) and open enrolment there is danger that a received curricula will prevail. The questions that must be asked are: where do colleagues have the opportunity for collaborative development? Will competition be the single motivating factor? Where will new ideas and thinking about curriculum and practice come from? Our own experience, professional judgement and evidence lead us to believe that partnership and collaboration is still a very significant motivator for raising quality in education. Tensions do exist between self-development, self-evaluation and centrally funded initiatives. It is vital, therefore, to look for the '*spaces between the contradictions*' in order to allow the principles of organic growth and individual development to take place in a climate of trust and professionalism. These tensions can be resolved if fundamental principles can be agreed and accepted, and if a conceptual framework is used to inform the actions and activities of the participants. If there is recognition that the exchange of ideas and a commitment to collaborative action are prerequisites for development it will be beneficial to forge new partnerships in the future and to support the growth of independent professional judgement. We need to recognise that the systems which encourage an atomisation of an educational service will not help to raise the quality of learning in our schools and colleges and it is as a contribution to this neglected area of debate that this chapter is addressed.

Notes

1   TVEI Extension in Hereford and Worcester began in September 1989 with the creation of six TVEI consortia. A total of 69 high schools, special schools and colleges are involved. The main purpose of the consortium structure is to enable planning, organisation and the deployment of

resources to be carried out efficiently and with flexibility. The management groups within each consortium provide the link between the central TVEI Unit and individual schools/colleges and are able to take account of local needs and circumstances. Two of the TVEI consortia began extension in September 1989 (Herefordshire and Worcester City) followed by four others in September 1990 (Bromsgrove, Redditch, South Worcester and Wyre Forest). A Curriculum Development Officer/TVEI Evaluator was appointed in June 1990 whose brief included the development of evaluation strategies.

The Evaluation Programme was established in order to support and evaluate curriculum developments within the LEA. The initial two years of the programme have been assisted by the Centre for Social Research in Education (CSRE) at the University of Keele whose staff have provided support, advice and in-service training. The programme is one of a number of initiatives involved in the LEA's drive towards the development of an 'evaluation culture' in the county. TVEI staff form part of the county co-ordinating group for evaluation and development activities.

2   During the initial phase of the evaluation programme a need was identified for support materials. A number of documents have been produced which set out the philosophy and structure of the evaluation programme. These include:

Evaluation in Schools and Colleges — An Introductory Guide
The 'Introductory Guide' attempts to set out some characteristics of formative evaluation stressing the importance of collaboration, of placing teaching and learning at the centre, and of considering the perspectives that may exist in a particular situation. The guide discusses the potential benefits of formative evaluation in terms of satisfying internal and external success criteria or performance indicators. Issues such as the 'Who?', 'What?' and 'How?' are also addressed.

A Framework for Evaluation
This working document provides a means of collecting data at various points during the programme. Information collected provides a basis for discussion, and for formative feedback. On completion the document acts as a record of the evaluation and contains data on which to base a short summative report.

Planning sheets, guidelines for report writing, and other papers are also available for use at various stages of the programme.

6 Building the Culture of Development in Schools and their LEA

Derek Glover and Tim Brighouse

THE CULTURE OF DEVELOPMENT I: SCHOOLS

Derek Glover

Twenty years ago it was not uncommon to find schools where the timetable ran from year to year with changes of staff or room but without fundamental consideration of the curriculum which was being delivered or the management of its delivery. The Head, usually acting alone, provided the subject structure for the school; the Certificate of Secondary Education (CSE) and O Levels provided the targets towards which the school worked and the examination boards were largely responsible for the content and so influenced the method of teaching; pedagogic skills were concerned with effective teaching to meet examination targets, and ability grouping ensured that the pupils 'knew where they stood, and where they were going'. Even at that time though, much was changing in many schools. McMullen (1970) demonstrated that the school could successfully develop in relation to its community and many schools were showing this responsiveness at the heart of their culture. Comprehensive reorganisation had removed many of the certainties upon which teaching had been based. Mixed ability groupings, learning support, relevant targets and the wholeness of the curriculum were being investigated as responses to the changed situation, and the overall effect was to undermine the stability of both the teaching and learning situations in schools. The Education Reform Act of 1988 may have put some brake on this development through the National Curriculum structure and content but there can be no return to the old times when the Head made the decisions and all acted accordingly. The management of National Curriculum delivery and assessment, open enrolment and the local management of schools requires a level of joint planning, co-operative action and shared responsibility which could not have been envisaged even in the most responsive school a decade ago.

The effect of these changes has been to encourage a greater degree of participation by the staff of schools. This is increasingly involving ancillary and support staff as school communities come to recognise their interdependence. It might be argued that the changes within schools have been imposed by the external environment. Certainly, the effects of legislation have caused a more rapid change in some schools. Increased efforts to integrate students with special learning needs, recognition of parental expression of preference, more open negotiation with parents and greater governor involvement have all prompted a developmental reaction in the schools. It can be demonstrated however, that the impetus for change was already present within the schools as the teaching staff recognised the deficiencies in what was being offered in the 1970s and as they strove to implement an increasing body of research findings which pointed to opportunities for a better education for all children. Plowden (1967) had been a catalyst for change in primary education, Rutter *et al.*, (1979) served as a prompt for secondary educators a decade later. Staff meetings became less 'niggle and natter', or a platform for the Head to address the troops, and, particularly after the development of in-service days in the last ten years, allowed opportunities for discussion of policy, whole school issues, cross-curricular themes, and management approaches in a more open manner than had been possible in the hierarchical, and subject constrained framework within which many staff were frustrated because they felt that they were not contributing either to meeting the needs of the individual pupil or the development of the school. Successful schools are flexible in the planning and membership of meetings recognising the dynamics of the school, and the varying needs of policy and practice from time to time.

It must not be thought that effective schools are an invention of the last decade. Tyerman (1968) in an analysis of the causes of truancy highlighted the need for a positive atmosphere rather than the more repressive regimes of many schools. The reputation of forward looking schools has long been a matter for community discussion. The early days of comprehensive reorganisation were accompanied by much innovative work both in teaching approaches and in management systems and strategies — records of achievement, negotiated targets, a broad and relevant curriculum, and attention to equal opportunities can all be traced to schools which were responding to need in their own way. The features which characterised them then are comparable with those which are evident in our most successful schools today. In brief, these relate to the nature of leadership, the development of shared values within the school community, and the fostering the ability of the school to recognise and respond to the environment.

Leadership

Despite the popular myth which elevates the Head to a higher plane, good leaders do not necessarily have to be charismatic personalities. They have, however, to recognise their own strengths and weaknesses and to plan the development of their school in such a way that complementary strengths are brought into being either through new appointments or through the provision of training opportunities for existing staff. This must spring from a vision of where the school is going and some ideas of the ways in which the vision can become a reality. Increased collegiality, discussed fully in Bush (1989), has developed from industrial practice in interpretation of the vision but can gain much more in a climate where professionalism is more important than status. It is significant that the students and staff in one small secondary school can all say that 'the school is to enable each and every one to reach their potential . . . and to enjoy the process' — the vision provides the criteria for all policy development. Within that school, though, it also means that differentiated learning, a flexible curriculum organisation, assessment, recording and negotiation are all seen as whole school issues and, whilst there may be some difference of approach between subjects, the partnership between students and staff is fundamental to relationships. 'How can there be enjoyment if a youngster has no opportunity to express views or staff are frustrated because they cannot be sure that somebody within the management structure does not understand their problems?'

The vision has to be translated into action. Especially in the larger schools roles and responsibilities are usually clearly defined. This requires the leadership to exercise true delegation if problems are to be avoided, and requires the led to accept that the buck may stop at a level lower down the management structure than the deputy or a Head. Unless something is drastically wrong, the person who is carrying the responsibility must be allowed to plan, act, make mistakes, evaluate and react without interference. The art of successful leadership lies in recognition of the point at which intervention becomes necessary. In one school this was expressed as follows: 'I know that I have got to cope with the problems of youngsters off-site at lunch time and that I may need help, so I am putting together some ideas after discussion with the other staff involved and I will then go to the Head with solutions as well as problems'. The postholder understands her role and responsibilities, she knows when to ask for help, she has sought the views of others in facing the problem and she knows that there will be a receptive ear for the proposed solutions. The leader has provided the atmosphere within which the vision can be maintained.

This also says a great deal about the way in which the leader is managing the human resources of the organisation. Recognition of the need to motivate others, often through the provision of opportunities to contribute to the collective debate or to feel especially valued appears to be fundamental to effective development work. One school, faced with the dilemma of National Curriculum implementation demonstrated many aspects of successful human resources management. The key to success was that in the year before any change was implemented all the staff agreed to contribute to eight working parties on cross-curricular themes. All working parties were given a small, but valued, time allocation and a support budget to allow them to plan their own visits, arrange visiting speakers and information technology back-up. The individual members of the working parties carried responsibility for elements of investigation and reporting and were given specific opportunities to negotiate at subject based meetings so that there was a whole school awareness of what was underway. Proposals were then taken to a reconstituted management consultative committee which effectively agreed priorities for the coming year within the resources available and detailed planning was then undertaken by the senior staff according to their executive responsibilities. Despite the minority view that the staff were having to take some decisions which the Head should have been taking, there was a general feeling that all staff were contributing to the development in a planned way which ensured participation, recognition and responsibility. The changes were then introduced when all the policy implications had been discussed — 'nobody could say that they hadn't been involved from the start'. In another school where succession planning has become the basis of professional development, inservice training and interschool co-operation, the Head felt that the key to staff motivation was that 'he always finds a bit of money to provide some wine and nibbles, and a bit of time so that we feel appreciated'.

'Shared Values'

In each of the schools mentioned there is a common acceptance of the 'shared values' by which the school lives, to the point that staff loyalty is an obvious feature of the school. This may involve recognition of staff opinion irrespective of position or status; it may be developed through social activities, mutual support or more formalised line management systems; it may hinge on the interpretation of the vision of the school or simply on institutional loyalty, and it may be related to an indefinable group chemistry which binds a group together adapting over time but still concerned with 'the way we do things here'.

There is a possibility that such cohesiveness could inhibit development by its very 'chumminess' but the evidence suggests that in schools where there is staff stability, where the pattern of relationships is open, known and supportive, and where trust is enhanced, change is less threatening. The story of the wrecking of a complete reorganisation of science teaching in one school because one of the seventeen staff involved refused to teach facing north may be apocryphal but it does point to the need for recognition of the fact that in any organisation there may come a point when the needs of the clients (in this case the students) may be thwarted by a refusal on the part of one member of staff to accept the norms and ideals of the team. Management, at this stage, will already have invoked patient negotiation, persuasion and attempted compromise and may need finally, to use coercion. Once again leadership consists of knowing when this time has come.

The extent to which such action can create bad feelings within the staff room depends on the common knowledge of all stages of the consultation process, awareness of the long term implications of failure to pursue an agreed policy, and the way in which interpersonal conflict has been managed. Where the team is strong, the objectives of the school are accepted by all, and fair dealing is known to exist, difficult decisions, can be palatable.

Problems are seen to develop where, although staff loyalty is strong, subgroup loyalties may be stronger. The days of the 'departmental barons' or the 'Napoleonic year head' appear to have been numbered since local management of schools imposed the need for a much greater degree of collective decision making. In one school, the decisions which cannot be readily agreed are placed before a management group which has elected representatives from the pastoral and academic structures at all stages of career development; in another, the sole criterion for decision making is how it accords with prioritisation as outlined in the school development plan; in another, the Head is sole arbiter but by the same token, carries all the opprobrium which might result; and in another, the matter under discussion is referred back to the relevant staff committee until a decision can be reached at that level. Whatever method is used it appears to be important to minimise those actions which might isolate colleagues or create a situation where no face saving is possible. One Head expressed this as 'the need to recognise that a consistent course of action will be followed and decisions will then be adhered to without favour of any sort'.

One school, having developed confidence through team teaching approaches over the last decade, and recognising the importance of team building, either in department, years or cross-curricular groups, asked all colleagues to agree to psychometric testing which enabled the identification of the skills which each individual member of staff could bring to group dynamics. As a result, the Head no longer chairs the senior management meetings, the science faculty is chaired by a younger member of staff with an A incentive post, and the alignment of groups within the Design and Performing Arts has been changed so that there is a balance of contributing strengths in each faculty. The comment from one member of staff that this constitutes psychological manipulation may have some validity but it is refreshing to meet staff who are prepared to use this knowledge of themselves not only in team building but also in their approaches to appraisal. Another school having made a similar attempt, with staff co-operation, to identify the strengths and weaknesses which each individual brings to corporate activity has recognised the dynamic nature of the school and reviews all structures every two years. Some staff comment that this leads to too much instability but the majority believe that it encourages adaptability, response to changing pressures and the involvement of all staff in this work. The hidden benefit is that there is a wider spread of incentive posts and a degree of flexibility in their use — 'We are valued for our contribution, not for who we are or what our salary status is'.

Shared values are not the prerogative of staff alone and effective schools appear to have developed systems which allow students to make their contribution to discussion of school organisation. This may be through the use of opportunities in personal and social education, it may be through school democracies based upon student councils, or it may be an atmosphere of open discussion in which staff provide opportunities for student contribution to debate. In an otherwise highly successful school, failure to maintain a consistent level of negotiation resulted in the imposition of a new school badge with a requirement that it be purchased by all students whatever the length of time remaining until they left the school. Student reaction reflected their horror at the way the change had been handled and provided evidence of the strength of student feeling once participation has been encouraged. 'I couldn't believe the staff would let it happen . . . they have always talked to us about the things which concern us . . . I wonder whether they have given up trusting our opinion . . . it isn't the way to make us feel that we count as members of the school community that we are always hearing about'. [Interview with Alistair, Year 11]. If student opinion is seen as an influence on development it must clearly be consistently sought, responded to and acted on within a reporting back system. In schools where this element of the partnership is fostered there seems to be less of a problem as a result of student disillusionment, but participation in a rich programme of activities, in which staff-student relationships are both natural and within known boundaries, also appears to provide a means of building upon those shared values by which the staff build school loyalty.

The External Environment

Whatever the nature of the leadership style, or its interpretation in the spirit of the school, there are increasing pressures for schools to recognise, and relate to their external environment. In a survey of 'community relationships' in an urban fringe, 11–16 comprehensive school, during a one week period at the end of the spring term, there were no fewer than 530 community contacts through work experience, classes shared with adults, an elderly persons activity afternoon, support for assemblies and social education, learning support, and participation in an industrial conference. The curriculum co-ordinator commented 'despite the strictures of the National Curriculum we have recognised that we need to use community resources and experience if we are to show the school to the community and, at the same time, provide a relevant experience for our youngsters'.

Awareness of these opportunities appears to facilitate development within schools. This may happen in several ways. The greater the involvement the greater the degree of understanding — the school described above has several people on the waiting list to become governors as opportunity arises. Parents are more ready to come onto the site, to negotiate for themselves or their children and to be more open and honest in their discussions with staff. Discipline problems have diminished as students have established improved relationships with local adults and as local adults have made use of school facilities; 'seeing the kids in their own setting showed they weren't so bad' was one comment. Open dialogue with community groups, agencies, potential employers and parents has enhanced the opportunities for supportive understanding of what the school is about. One school has illustrated this by referring the negotiation of a system of records of achievement to as many of the local community as possible to ensure that the personal interests, work experience, and community involvement sections were realistic in their demands and fair in their assessment.

Consideration of the consultative structures operating within effective schools suggests that recognition of the view of staff and students is often enhanced by the use of additional advisory groups. The Governors, although their policy making role is legally paramount, have an important role in consultation because they may represent the diversity of interests in the immediate environment. Parental participation, traditionally through fundraising for the school, has been enhanced through the development of meetings with an educational theme and discussion of policy issues — there are several examples of their involvement in assessment of the strengths of the school. The community at large may be similarly involved either through an extension of the parental participation outwards to the friends of the school, through advisory groups as used in some schools for industrial liaison or the evolution of a community curriculum, or, in the most developed stage, as participants in the management of a community education programme.

The cost of all this is however, that the school has to become open to comment and criticism from those who may not understand philosophy or practice within the school.

The Evaluation Process

This points to the need for schools which are prepared to be open in their relationships to have an evaluation process which enables them to recognise and respond to constructive criticism. Traditionally this may have come about because of a comment made by a governor at a meeting, or by a complaint from a local resident or because of expressed unease by a group of staff, but it was a somewhat hit and miss affair leading to pragmatic action independent of overall policy. In the past decade evaluation has become more systematic and used as an essential part of development rather than to produce instant reaction. It was realised that HMI inspections and county inspectoral visits were both external to the school and likely to be based on criteria which might relate to county or national perceptions of what the school should be about. In several education authorities schools were encouraged to establish their own system of evaluation and materials have been provided to help with this process as shown in the Guidelines for the Review and Internal Development of Schools or the University of Bath *Signposts to Self-Evaluation*. The culture of evaluation was fostered by the organisation of the Technical and Vocational Education Initiative which gave schools self-set targets against which they could measure progress. Initially, self-evaluation was all embracing as shown in the 300 page reports produced by some schools. Over time the work has become more focused, often with an agreement between school and LEA to concentrate on some issues as part of an authority wide initiative together with some which are particular to the school.

Initially, self-evaluation appeared to be largely descriptive, often presenting excuses for problems outlined and was frequently used as a rod to beat the backs of those responsible for resourcing schools. There is considerable evidence to suggest that schools now see evaluation as a means of informing their own response to problems through recognition of the process of data collection, analysis, posing solutions, action and review. One school, to use its self-evaluation most effectively, considers every agreed item over a two year period so that this process can be linked to the school development plan. The termly review meetings are regarded as target setting sessions where progress towards development plan aims can be monitored. Schools in which self-evaluation is well developed report a change in attitude on the part of staff 'from the suspicious to the collaborative, from bland acceptance to seeking an explanation for phenomena, and from believing that nothing can be changed to seeking ways of achieving the impossible' [Deputy Head, Group 5, 13–18 school]. Another school reports that staff are more willing to share ideas and to look at alternative approaches to learning styles as a result of the way in which evaluation at departmental level has been achieved by building upon the ideas of joint responsibility for the progress of each department towards self-set targets. In both the schools there has been an informal appraisal system for the past three years which, in the words of one professional development co-ordinator, 'shows how far we have gone along the road of being honest with each other about the contribution we make to the youngsters' success'.

Readiness to be self-critical, respond to requests for data and observation and to contribute to cross-curricular development all appear to grow from awareness of the evaluative process. It is significant that much in-service time has been given to the presentation of coping strategies which help to ensure the success of the process although many staff initially resent time spent on process rather than product. In one school this has been expressed as 'an example of the way in which our thought processes have changed as we learnt that it was the doing that was as important as what we produced'. The danger is that the product then becomes ignored. To counteract this, one school has insisted that each evaluation exercise has a timetabled life with clear reporting of the data, action planning, implementation and reappraisal stages resulting in a growing file of evaluative reports. Another, much smaller school, has evolved a system which is based on investigation groups drawn from staff, parents, governors and community who are given the task of producing a report for guidance within a six month time allocation. The important feature of these two approaches is that the evaluation is for a purpose and forms the basis of action.

Evaluation as the Basis of Development

Mention has been made of 'action planning' as the basis of development work within schools. If evaluation has been fostered through supportive and open leadership, a spirit of togetherness in the approach to problems and the inculcation of skill in dispassionate assessment of progress toward aims, then action planning is the way forward because it links into the developmental processes for the institution. This is exemplified in one large high school where the development plan is crafted in the following way. Each member of staff, after discussion with his or her line manager, produces a self-evaluation sheet which outlines perceived needs in individual development, ability to contribute to the work of the department, and ability to contribute to the cross-curricular themes currently given priority within the school. These sheets are compared with the departmental development sheets which list priorities for the coming three year period, and the whole school working party sheets which review cross-curricular priorities. From this work it is possible to programme a development plan for the school which records personal, subject and whole school targets and needs. This is then considered by a management team drawn from all sections of the staff and governors to achieve a detailed programme for the coming year and an outline of intent for the following two years. 'The value is that we all know what we need, we all see how it fits into the total programme and we all know that there has been fairness in the allocation of resources and time to ensure that priorities are both integrated and achieved' [Head of Department]. The process does not stop at the programming because the work of each autumn term is taken with an assessment of the ways in which the development planning for the previous education year has been achieved. Again this involves individuals, subject departments and cross-curricular groups all of whom contribute to the assessment sheets which are then used as additional material for the consideration of priorities in current planning.

The process, especially when described in brief appears to be very time consuming but after three years the staff report that it enables them to establish professional and teaching needs, to programme developments according to those needs, and to assess progress without the need for external intervention. The school has used county advisory staff and governors as critical friends in the process but does not consider them to be 'outside'. It may be thought that the system is slow in that instantaneous reaction is inhibited because of the need to go through the assessment and action process, and that the implied collegiality asks more of the staff than the former system where priorities were decided by a Court of Star Chamber consisting of the Head and Deputies. Response is, however, considered and essential changes achieved within a year of the assessment review. This is shown in that after two years of concentration on individual training, curriculum planning and implementation for cross-curricular themes it became obvious that there was need for a return to subject priorities in order to meet the needs of National Curriculum and revised assessment. This was accepted as the basis for the immediate year's action plan and staff and governors recognise that further assessment might indicate that this should continue as a priority for another year or more.

In all this the question of 'assessment against what criteria' is a widespread concern. The move to more objective data in assessment processes has led schools to investigate the performance indicators suggested by TVEI, by the DES Aide Memoire of 1989, and by local authorities. Those schools which have a well developed evaluation and planning system appear to have settled upon their own system of data collection. One uses the value added concept by considering the progress of all students against the admission data at the end of years 9 and 11; another asks each department and year team to provide standardised information agreed at a staff meeting for that purpose; another sets the 'pointers' for investigation each year and then collects the information on the 'markers' achieved at the end of the review period, and yet another relies on each organisational group to evolve its own criteria for assessment according to its needs in the interpretation of the school development plan. Whatever system is used it seems that the ready acceptance by the staff of the need to evaluate and the way in which progress can be charted is essential for success. In the words of one member of staff 'the indicators are our way of getting the information we need to see how we are doing . . . I don't see the data as a threat because it can be such a help to have some fact to back your hunches.

The Way Ahead

Enabling styles of leadership, open discussion and awareness of the needs and expectations of client groups appear to create the atmosphere within which staff are prepared to evaluate and plan. Present indications are that many of the functions previously undertaken by the LEA advisory or inspection services will be undertaken within the school using their own resources backed up by 'consultative' help as needed. To assist with this many authorities have developed self-evaluation and school development planning strategies which can be adapted to individual school needs. It is evident that many schools recognise this support and it might be helpful to conclude this section by reference to one school where the evaluative structure is based on assessment techniques for listed features of school philosophy and practice, the results of which can then be incorporated into development planning. Each feature is considered with descriptors at four levels — awareness of the need, evidence of policy discussion, school implementation planning and ongoing evaluation.

Where features are undeniably at level four and integrated into the review process of the school Fullan's (1982) 'embedding' has taken place and change has been achieved but at all other levels there is more work to be undertaken in the development of that feature in the practice of the school. Initial analysis of homework policies in one school, and of negotiated learning in another suggest that there may be some advantage in this approach which not only sets the standards for the school as a whole but which also gives a prompt to individual staff concerned with the maintenance and development of their contribution to the life of the school. Awareness of this appears to be fundamental to successful development planning that lies at the heart of school improvement.

THE CULTURE OF DEVELOPMENT II: LEAS — THEIR INFLUENCE ON SCHOOL CULTURE

Tim Brighouse

History gives us one set of messages about the influence of LEAs on the culture of schooling: the present has ushered in a new set of demands with a different emphasis. How far either provides a guide for future action is something I shall consider at the chapter's end.

The issue itself is enigmatic. The capacity of an LEA to affect the outcome of school is one of the least researched aspects of education. Legend abounds but there are precious few facts.[1]

Among the professionals in the education service there are, of course, legendary figures. Sharpe and then Alexander both Chief Education Officers (CEOs) in Sheffield were thought to be directive and influential: indeed, Christopher Price, Director of the Metropolitan University of Leeds, says that in the Sheffield of his youth, Alexander would summon to a private inquisition hapless headteachers of Sheffield primary schools where the results in the 11 + were below par. Spurley Hey and Fisher were two great Directors of Education in Manchester and there were the Taylors in Leeds. Such men, there were no women, driven by the examples found within their own education from classical Greece and Rome, sought the creation of a civilised society.

Outside the great conurbations there were small county boroughs and 'excepted districts' before local government reorganisation. There too emerges anecdotal evidence of distinguished begowned figures — the Directors of Education — visiting the local grammar school in the 1930s to deliver an annual lecture intended to raise the aspirations of the next generation of citizens. But there are also stories in the same places of nepotism and parochialism which were manifest in the appointment system. Aldermen and women used to feel that they had powers of patronage. In exercising such powers, they were doubtless exhibiting what they would have seen as a very natural extended familial concern for the sons and daughters of local citizens. Even today, in Wales, Scotland, the Midlands and the North, there is a natural propensity for teachers to return to teach. Nevertheless the legacy in some parts of the country bears witness to the long hand of yesterday's practices reaching out to touch the culture even of schooling today as the parochialism so encouraged also limited vision and new ideas — an antidote to curriculum development and intellectual curiosity.

Such was never the fate of London. The multicultural nature of the community, the poverty, and the challenge of waves of new immigrants, meant that the capital city, from the beginning of the century in the London School Board and later through the LCC and ultimately the ILEA, became a crucible in which the ablest of each successive generation of teachers forged progressive practice in the face of sometimes apparently insuperable difficulties.

In the shire counties it was yet again somewhat different. Although the legendary Martin Wilson, Chief Education Officer in pre and post-war Shropshire, has a reputation for having fashioned a community where educational development was encouraged, counties for the most part were places where long lines of communication and the ubiquitous influences of the churches and the squirearchy meant that the seasons came and went with blessed certainty.

Mostly, however, there was a *laissez-faire* attitude to the quality of schools' performance. All LEAs, urban and rural, were more concerned with quantity than quality.

There were, after all, schools to be built to accommodate the shift from allage to separate primary and secondary schools before and after the 1939–45 war. There were successive rises in the school leaving age to implement. Later there were the colleges of further education to develop, adult education centres to establish, youth clubs to create, new schools to plan and design for successive population explosions. Of course, as we shall see, how the buildings were designed especially in the 1960 to 1975 period, when there was massive expansion to build to meet a population bulge, could affect the culture and practice of schools, but the influence there was more from the DES than individual LEAs. In any case, the post-war period, until at least the late 1960s and early 1970s, was one where education was regarded as an uncomplicated and 'good thing'. The curriculum was identified in 1962 as 'a secret garden' by Sir David Eccles, the then Minister of Education, but for years nothing much was really done to disturb the gardeners. Quite simply there was no encouragement for the LEA to think that it should influence the culture of schooling.

Probably the student unrest of 1968 which followed closely on the heels of the last of the great reports (Plowden) from the Central Advisory Council and coincided with the publication of the Black Papers, should have alerted LEAs to the need to pay more attention to the development of quality and to the need for more accountability. Local government reorganisation, however, occupied the minds and time of educationalists and politicians for the next five years. Then LEAs were into a period which demanded further attention to quantitative rather than qualitative matters — namely falling school rolls and chronic economic crisis.

So the background of LEA influence on the quality of schooling is unpromising. Moreover, it wasn't until the late 1970s that HMI published their document 'Ten Good Schools' and Rutter his book 'Fifteen Thousand Hours' based on research into school effectiveness. The understanding of the subtle ways in which LEAs might consciously influence the culture and assumptions of schooling was a rare commodity in earlier years. Sadly, it took nearly a decade for the lessons of Rutter and HMI to inform the actions of LEAs and by then it was too late.

As I have implied, there was some accidental or unintended influence but most LEAs did not intentionally set out to exercise any. There are, however, some genuine exceptions. They relate to the influence of a few Chief Education Officers. I have already mentioned Martin Wilson in Shropshire. Some other distinguished ones come to mind. Henry Morris, in Cambridgeshire, influenced events by ideas which he advocated with some eloquence. Morris was a person keenly aware of the power of imagery and ideas in language and art. He used them and the buildings to influence the culture of schooling. In doing so he was tirelessly promoting the concept of the 'village college' and he gave it physical expression by the employment of great architects. Gropius, for example, designed Impington Village College. Sir John Newsom followed a similar strategy as CEO in Hertfordshire. He sought to influence the environment, not so much by the school architecture, although he regarded it as important, as by introducing works of art to new school buildings. Henry Moore, for example, created the powerful sculpture at the entrance to Barclay School in Stevenage. Both Newsom and Leicestershire's CEO, Stewart Mason, who was also keenly appreciative of the potent influence of the interplay of art and the building environment, went slightly further. They, to a greater extent than Morris, were talent spotters determined to find men — it was an era long before the adoption of ideas of equality for women — for key appointments. In doing so they were consciously seeking to influence school culture.

The Chief Education Officer who generously or grudgingly was regarded by others as the one who pre-eminently thought about affecting the culture of schooling was Alec Clegg in the West Riding. He went after his man, was alive to the buildings and the environment and led the way with ideas, words and imagery. But he had other skills in his repertoire. As a manager of educational change who appreciated the potential coherence of LEA power, Clegg was a person far ahead of his time. In politics, Machiavelli would have enjoyed him; in practice, his influence remained so great that in March 1992, about twenty years after his retirement, it was possible for me to pick up unprompted conversation about Clegg's educational ideas and their influence on present daily practice by young teachers in one of the former West Riding schools. So what extra did he do? Certainly and crucially he linked initiatives so that they reinforced each other. In doing so he found ways of applying compound interest to their effect. So the potential of using money to influence change in the curriculum was first exploited by Clegg. Advisers, carefully chosen on the basis of a shared philosophy and value system, were able to reinforce the changes of approach encouraged by head-hunted appointments to the leadership of schools. Advisers achieved such an outcome by dispensing small sums of money made available to support certain changes and, by implication, not others. In Clegg's West Riding, a thousand flowers certainly bloomed but unlike other places the varieties were not entirely random.

A gift for publicity enabled extensive numbers of teachers and support staff in the West Riding enterprise to feel part of a nationally, even internationally, significant development. In the end national initiatives were influenced by Clegg's thinking rather than vice-versa.

One of the other techniques Clegg introduced was the power not so much of the adviser but of the advisory teacher or coach. The latter technique is best illustrated perhaps by a closer consideration of another county authority.

Allan Chorlton, Oxfordshire's Chief Education Officer, was a shy and somewhat remote figure with singular ideas and a determination to see that others shared them. He appointed an officer, later called an adviser/organiser, Edith Moorhouse, a tough lady from Yorkshire who was aided and abetted by two HMIs, Robin Tanner, an etcher, and Len Comber, a mathematician, who together systematically attempted to transform primary schools. Her method was simple: she appointed three or four advisory teachers and ensured that she overcame the natural isolation of the teacher within the school and of the schools themselves, by bringing them together after school and at weekends to discuss their good practice. The advisory teachers who tended to stay in post for a decade or more, busied themselves during the day quietly, by spending weeks at a time working in school alongside teachers, building relationships founded on natural trust and respect, and sharing difficulties, triumphs and good practice by encouraging learning and talking together. Comber and Tanner were the inspiration and the validators of what went on. Ideally, teachers were expected to be artists, writers, craftsmen and women in their own right: youngsters in schools became researchers as well as vessels to be filled with useful information. Edith Moorhouse's successor, John Coe, came from the West Riding in 1969: indeed, Oxfordshire's files show that they looked to the West Riding for a successor because the officers were anxious to recruit someone in sympathy with their approach to primary education. The process was akin to a football club's scouting system: it was one which Coe himself pursued and which I copied as CEO of the same county from 1978 to 1989, in respect of recruitment for the county's secondary headteacher positions. In a sense it echoed the selection process established on a slightly more idiosyncratic basis, in John Newsom's Hertfordshire. Nor should its importance be underestimated. After all, by the 1980s governing bodies and representatives of the Education Committee were properly suspicious of a Chief Officer's nominee, so that the most one could do was ensure that particular candidates at least were looked at. Inevitably, there were some good people who slipped through the net and it was inevitable too, that some with impeccable pedigree apparently suited to a particular task, in practice didn't live up to expectations. That in a sense is not the point. What the process illustrates is a way in which LEAs could influence the leadership of schools — a factor which all the research suggests is a vital ingredient in school effectiveness. That ability has been largely removed as a result of the 1988 Education Act and there seems to be no systematic attempt to enable the benefits of such practice to be perpetuated. Indeed, the emergence of equal opportunity employment policies in the late 1980s in any case put the system at risk. In their most rigorous application, such schemes tipped the balance of advantage in favour of each applicant getting a fair crack of the whip which was sometimes at the expense of the school to which they were appointed. This is not surprising since the match of appropriate qualities, skills and competencies to the individual needs of a particular school is, at best, a delicate and elusive judgement. Heads, successful in one set of circumstances, are not in another: persons suitable for one stage of a school's development are not for the next. Equal opportunity and employment practices do not allow for such subtleties. Differential advice and consideration of candidates is often eschewed in an infuriating propensity for people to confuse equal opportunity with providing the same thing for everyone. Now there is something worse looming. Inexperienced governing bodies are more rather than less likely to appoint internal candidates.

It is worth pausing on the 'working alongside' model of advisory teacher work pioneered in a few post-war LEAs. I describe

Oxfordshire because I could see the long-term fruits of its application, but the same practice informed the West Riding, Leicestershire and Bristol. A subsequent derivative of the model had a brief outing in the last days of the Inner London Education Authority. David Hargreaves' report for ILEA 'Improving Secondary Schools' (1985), first rehearsed the arguments for Inspectors Based in Schools (IBIS) — an initiative aimed principally at secondary schools, where it was expected that Inspectors working alongside teachers and sharing in the daily life of the school, would provide extra time and expertise in order to improve practice. There is precious little evidence to illuminate the efficacy of the initiative because it was simply one among the many measures which Hargreaves then found himself as the leader of the ILEA Inspectorate trying to implement. Indeed, by the time of abolition, only a modest start had been made. Perhaps in modern times and especially in London, it is more difficult to replicate the stability and longevity in post which was a feature of the advisory teacher post in Oxfordshire. Longevity and stability of personnel moreover were not features of the advisory teacher initiatives associated first of all with the 'Mathematics Missionaries' initiatives funded by Sir Keith Joseph, the Secretary of State, under the Education Support Grant (ESG) arrangements following Cockcroft's report on mathematics, nor of the brief rash of LEA initiatives as they responded to the ending of the INSET pooling scheme and the introduction first of GRIST (Grant Related Inservice Training) and then LEATGS (Local Education Authority Training Grant Scheme). It was little wonder that such a rapid expansion gave advisory teachers a bad name, for it was inevitable that they would attract to their ranks people who were the very antithesis of those advisory teachers in Oxfordshire in the immediate post-war years.

Nevertheless, the function of the respected professional working alongside teachers and bringing with them the daily experience of working in apparently similar but different situations in other schools, is an important one and potentially a powerful influence. The practice of it over many years in Oxfordshire was obvious. There was a shared value system which spread far beyond a few individual schools. Some of the features of that belief were evident in a curriculum which was at once designed to respond to a multi-faceted view of intelligence while at the same time emphasising the importance of first hand experience in small research tasks. These were designed to train the child in scientific method demanding of them powers of systematic observation, the collection of evidence, the discriminating sifting of that evidence and the drawing of conclusions from the process, together with the writing up and often — perhaps to excess — the visual representation of the work or a part of the exercise. In consequence, whole schools were meticulous in the way they exhibited all their children's work. There was a discernible Oxfordshire style of display subtly different from the West Riding. At its best, it not merely celebrated all rather than a few children, but also reflected a teacher's determination to use the walls as supplementary educators in matters affecting language, maths, science, and the environment and would often include examples of unfinished work or puzzles to prompt the observer's mind. There were other features too. There was for example an extraordinary and pervasive practice of using Italian Florentine script as a handwriting model. The locality perhaps in consequence boasts among its adult population a prolific number of practising calligraphers. There seemed to be no orthodoxy however as to reading and other teaching methods. Headteachers, advisers and teachers were in the main bound together by a similar set of values and they knew where to attract to their ranks replacements. Colleges in York, Ripon and Lincoln were regarded as favourites, as later was Charlotte Mason in Ambleside: these were all places which could be relied upon to provide good teachers. Groups of children and their teachers would visit such colleges for residential experience.

The features — and there were many others — which I describe as noticeable and different on arrival in the county in the late 1970s were the outcome of thirty years of consistent reinforcement by the LEA.

I am not arguing the case here — though I would — for the validity of the particular philosophy and direction taken by successive generations of professionals. I am merely underlining that all LEAs could have exercised similar influences, especially in years when governors and managers had less power and were inclined to use it less often than they do today.

Apart from appointments and advisory teacher support, the LEAs who were determined to influence quality, frequently used whatever money they could scrape together for after school inservice courses in the evening or at weekends. In the early 1980s a few LEAs exploited the uncapped pool in order to create twenty day courses, one term opportunities or one year secondments for groups of teachers in order to develop the quality of schooling. It was a brief golden era where the LEA could identify projects attractive to different groups of schools and enable three or four teachers from each of the interested schools to have to work together on something of importance to the school itself.

It is at least arguable — given the increased knowledge that was developing about school effectiveness — that by the second half of the 1980s there was a growing and more sophisticated and discerning capacity among LEA in the matter of developing the schools and their culture. They knew how important appointments, particularly to leadership, were and were taking steps to improve the appointment process. They had developed extensive inservice partnerships with providing universities, colleges and polytechnics. Some had appreciated the potent force of the advisory teacher. A few (Salford, Solihull, ILEA, Oxfordshire) had pioneered instruments of school self-evaluation and a smaller number still started collaborative school reviews involving parts of their advisory and/or inspectorate teams. Above all, in a few places, they had established a professional climate of debate with which a substantial proportion of their teachers identified.

What I hope I have illustrated so far is that LEAs until the late 1980s, had they but known it, had amazing powers to influence the culture of schooling. They may be summarised as follows:

- Deciding where and in what form schools would be built. Architectural design and internal layout could be influenced by their philosophy with consequences for subsequent teaching practice.
- Influencing the appointment of headteachers and others.
- Directing the budgets of individual schools.
- Supplementing the budgets to link curriculum developments.
- Providing targeted inservice.
- Appointing and directing advisers and inspectors.
- Publicising their activities.

The 1988 Education Act, together with other legislation, affecting local government has changed that. The analysis of the potential for influence is not invalidated — influencing appointments, affecting the professional discourse, inservice arrangements, affecting the environment and planning of new schools, are all powerful agents of change. It is how and whether the LEA can exercise these functions and whether there are new ones that is now worth consideration.

At first the 1988 Education Act seemed to reinforce the powers of LEA to monitor evaluate and inspect. Encouraged by the Audit Commission's paper 'Losing an Empire and Finding a Role'[2] many LEAs enthusiastically set about laying greater emphasis on their powers of inspection, monitoring and evaluation. There was a recasting of practices of inspection which led most LEAs, for the first time, to realise their powers to influence school culture by 'joint reviews' by 'day visits', by 'curriculum audits' and by various other combinations of these practices. In the main, in the earlier years, only the ILEA had an extensive practice in this respect.

The Education Bill of 1992, however, besides removing substantial powers of provision and planning, snatched some of this new power away for it aimed to introduce the same principle of compulsory competitive tendering to the schools' use of inspection, which had been earlier applied to so many other local government services. Despite alterations in the House of Lords, it not only separates inspection from advisory functions but also removes the money to enable inspections to be made from the LEAs. It has effectively separated powers of purchase from powers of provision. Moreover, the other features of the earlier 1988 Education Act itself, for example, the squeeze on centrally provided parts of the school budget under the rules to be applied to the LMS formula; the removal of further education from local government; the encouragement of grant maintained schools; all conspired to weaken the LEA. Indeed, the influence of central government on schools had shifted the balance of power towards central government itself. The Secretary of State effectively sets the agenda and directs the vital expenditure at the margin by the use of earmarked grants. Central government too has determined the nature of the curriculum and the assessment arrangements after securing reports from quangos (NCC and SEAC) which it itself has appointed.

The challenge is how these, in many ways, unpromising arrangements the new LEA can still influence the quality and direction in schools.

It is important to emphasise the 'new' as a qualification to the LEA not merely to underline that so many of the lessons of the past cease to apply in the world after the 1988 Education Act and the two Acts of 1992, but also to remind ourselves of the fact that there is to be another reform of local government. It seems certain that outside the metropolitan districts there will be the complication of all LEAs being reformed into a larger number of unitary authorities, perhaps in the longer term within a regional framework. (It may be argued that regional government is something which was only considered by the Labour Party but the outcome of the debates following European realignment and the knock on effects on changes in Scotland and Wales may well force some reconsideration of some form of planning in government above the unitary authority and below Whitehall).

What then will the recast LEA be able to do to influence school culture? First, it will be wise to analyse what real powers they have: it may be helpful to use a matrix.

Figure 6.1   Local education authorities functions

	Pre-five	**Schools**	**Post-16**
Managing Functions Planning Providing Maintaining Monitoring			
Regulating Functions Monitoring Evaluating			
Promoting and Advocacy Communicating			

Amongst these the key decision is at what point the LEA as a provider, wishes to place itself on the minimalist/monopolist continuum. The nearer an LEA chooses to adopt the minimalist position the further it will distance itself from being able to apply the lessons of the old LEAs. On the other hand, its ability to influence through promotion, advocacy and the publication of information, will be considerable.

Whatever the future, the LEA sets the budget. Unless there is a move for central government to impose some form of uniform age weighted pupil unit, individual LEAs will affect the budgets even of grant maintained schools. In setting the budget the LEA could seek to debate with the heads and governors, including those of grant maintained schools, the basis on which it composes the budget. What pupil teacher ratio does it assume? How much does it expect to be spent on books and equipment? Is there a framework for non-teaching support staff? What are the assumptions about staff cover for absence and about contact time? What about its policies and funding practices for special educational need?

It will be within the interest of governors, heads and staff to want to argue the realism of the LEA's assumptions about all these questions but, the nature of that debate and the monitoring of the pattern of outcomes of expenditure in all the individual schools, could ultimately be powerfully influential on the practice of individual schools. A scheme operated like that on national level in the mid-1970s between the DES and representatives of the Local Authorities and the expenditure steering group (education) will commend itself. The important difference will be that whereas at a national level with over 30,000 schools and 103 LEAs (as there were then) and with the added complication of the rate support grant distribution formula encompassing not just educational expenditure but that for social services, fire, police, housing and so on, it was never going to be very influential. But most of those circumstances won't obtain so far as a purely schools grant to institutions is concerned, especially where that grant's sole purpose is to spend the designated budget for the intended purpose. If the preliminaries to that debate each year incorporate the opportunity for a well publicized professional debate about the comparative merits of different priority choices, the LEAs could have more influence than perhaps they imagine on individual schools especially if they were to use their centrally retained marginal funds wisely and publicly.

Moreover, in the mechanics of the LMS distribution system, LEAs will be able to influence schools powerfully towards inclusive rather than exclusive practices if they wish. That is particularly so in the way they treat and fund through the age weighted pupil unit, pupils with special educational needs. Those choices and those influences are therefore available for LEAs to exercise.

Finally, the outcomes, providing they are few in number which the LEA chooses to highlight in its monitoring processes, will also influence over a period the actions of teachers in most schools.

In short, in the future LEAs will still be able to influence the climate in which schools operate. Indeed, given the LEAs loss of power to central government and to schools, it seems likely that they will be tenacious in exercising what influence remains. If they have ceased to be the planner, provider, organiser and a maintainer, they will be very anxious to be advocate promoter and a defender of justice.

The enigma at the heart of this dilemma for the LEA of the future lies in the role of advisory and inspectorate services. It may well be that the combined impact of the 1992 Education Act and the moves encouraged by that and other legislation to divorce the purchaser and provider functions of local authorities will lead to the LEAs of the future providing a small core of advisers who commission or encourage the commission of fixed term consultancies in support of school development. After all 'four yearly' inspections required by law are going to induce a 'compliance' culture in schools which will need some alternative or complementary input. There are perhaps new alliances to be made in order to increase the influence that LEAs have. LEAs may well need to forge closer links with universities and colleges in order to optimise their influence in advisory work from the security of a sound research base. Perhaps, all professional staff of an LEA should be associates of the local faculty of education providing a base for a local branch of a general teaching council.

Essentially what LEAs have to face is that, after being the hand-maiden of a new arrangements affecting curriculum governance and management, their own role, if analyzed on the matrix provided earlier, is so transformed that nothing less than a cultural revolution will allow them to influence the culture of schooling. For the metropolitan LEAS that is a challenge to existing frameworks; for the counties, following the Local Government Commission, it will be the occasion to start again.

Notes

1   There are few accounts of LEA activity. A monograph on Martin Wilson's Shropshire is available from the Education Management Department of Sheffield Polytechnic. Harry Ree and Peter Jones wrote biographies of Henry Morris (Cambridgeshire) and Stewart Mason (Leicestershire) respectively. An analysis of the influence of local education authorities in Canada, the States and the UK is to be found in variously:

   (i)   FULLAN, M. (1991) *The New Meaning of Educational Change*, London, Cassell.
   (ii)   CLOUGH, E., ASPINWALL, K. and GIBBS, B (1991) *Learning to Change*, London, Falmer Press. (especially Chapter 9 'Implications for LEAs: the end of an era or the forerunner of a new?').
   (iii) BENTON, P. (1990) *The Oxford Internship Scheme*, Calouste Gulbenkian.

2   Audit Commission Occupational Paper No. 10 *Losing an Empire, Finding a Role: The LEA of the Future* (Dec 1989).

Both authors of this chapter have conducted research and provided consultancy advice for Hereford and Worcester LEA and its schools.

7 Using Critical Friends: Internalising the External

Colin Bayne-Jardine and Peter Holly

> Probably the most important single process involved in effective change is the process of **learning while doing**. The complexity of change strategies demands that processes of feedback and replanning make up the essential core of change management . . .
> Learning and change processes are part of each other. **Change is a learning process and learning is a change process**.

This passage by authors Beckhard and Pritchard (1992) is contained within a chapter entitled 'Creating a learning organization'. Senge (1990) has written about the Learning Organization in terms that are very similar. Moreover, Holly and Southworth (1989), have argued that a school can be the apotheosis of a learning organization: its 'business' is student learning and it is a good example of an organization that needs to learn — in order to change. Any learning organization, however, to merit that description, has to have a learning system. It has to have a way of learning which embraces both feedback information and the ability to act on the strength of this information. It is a case of effective information/data processing; it's a case of **action research**.

A learning organization (say, a school) needs an internal learning system (action research). Yet a school as a learning organization can also be embedded in a learning system. This 'system' is not a set of techniques or strategies (the learning system inside a school); it is the **systemic whole**. In education, this wider learning system can be the Local Education Authority. In the United States, there is much interest in the creation of a school district (the nearest equivalent to the LEA) as a learning system in which are embedded learning organizations (schools), each with its own individual learning system. Such a school district will need to have, it is argued, a learning culture.

It is the action research, says Holly (1992), that enables a system to have a system for learning. On-going reflection on action and action on reflection are the order of the day: learning by doing. Moreover, it is the action research that is not only the information/database for a system but also the vehicle for linkage within the system. In Bellevue Public Schools in Washington State, USA, action research is being conducted in classrooms and the schools and at the district level and all the participants are being networked and linked electronically. Therefore, it becomes possible for data to be created in one part of the system and used in other parts of the system. Data can be created for others to learn from. Previously, however, it has often been the case that district level data collected 'on' schools has been threatening to those schools and consequently remains ignored by them. Now, in Bellevue, the data collected by the local district researcher, Jan de Lacy, is not only being used by the schools to inform their action planning but, also, says de Lacy, is acting as a spur to those schools to collect their own data and to further research some of the issues emerging from her own work. This is fast-becoming a learning partnership. The work in Bellevue is also reflecting many of the characteristics of action research itself. As Holly and Anderson (1991) have underlined, action research is characterized by:

- participative data-gathering
- participative decision-making
- horizontalism, power-sharing and the relative suspension of hierarchical ways of working
- collaboration among group members acting as a critical community

Learning systems learn internally: it is learning from within — it has to be internalized. But learning systems can learn from the outside as long as the advice and guidance is presented sympathetically and with internal learning in mind. The learning system can be enhanced in its learning by the work of an effective **critical friend**. This person is external but has those internal at heart; he/she is: 'comfortable but challenging, challenging but not threatening' (Holly, 1991).

Elliot Eisner (1983) has described the nature of the role of the critical friend: (see Chapter One) and has concluded that a 'fresh eye', offered in a trusting relationship of 'joint reflection' leads to illumination and an 'integrated process' of professional (and school) development.

This is the role that Peter Holly has been fulfilling not only in the USA but also in Hereford and Worcester LEA. For several years he has been advising the LEA and its schools as a critical friend/process consultant, particularly in the areas of school development planning and school self-evaluation. His external perspective has added a 'fresh eye, distance and an illuminative intent' to the work in the Authority. Indeed, one of his focus areas has been helping schools with their needs assessment both by providing them with a range of skills that they can then use in a self-evaluative mode and by offering his external perspective using such a technique as **portraiture**.

Portraiture (see the work of Lightfoot (1983)) is a 'picture in words' painted by an outside observer and offered to the staff members of the recipient school for their reflection and illumination. Two examples of this approach-in-action are provided below. Both were constructed in similar fashion. The 'data' was gathered during an intensive one-day visit with two students acting as guides and mentors for the observer. Additional to the constant conversation with the students, the critical friend was able to conduct brief, informal interviews and make observation notes. Some background documentation was also made available. The reports were then constructed and delivered to the schools in the form of an oral presentation — in one case to the whole staff and in the other to the senior staff team. The intention of these meetings was to 'pass the baton' of ownership and awareness and to encourage the schools to build the reports into their thinking and action planning.

Two real-life examples of portraiture reports are offered.

CASE STUDY ONE: 'THE SCHOOL THAT CARES'

Foreword

This 'portraiture' of Pewton High School has been prepared by Peter Holly for general discussion inside the school as part of its institutional development planning process. It is based on a framework of four quadrants which are produced by interlinking two dimensions, the individual and the institution and development and maintenance (see below). As much as possible, the actual words of respondents have

Colin Bayne-Jardine and Peter Holly

Figure 7.1 *The basic framework*

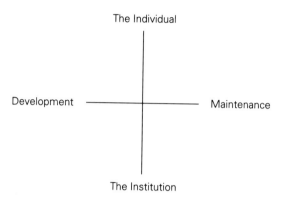

been included in the text. The idea of a portraiture is to provide a commentary by an external 'critical friend' in order to stimulate internal reflection and dialogue.

Introduction

> According to general indicators of health, we're doing very well.
>
> Headteacher

I would go further. I would say that Pewton High School shows every sign of being a healthy organisation; that is, a healthy educational organisation. While the size of the school is undoubtedly a factor, it is necessary but not sufficient in explaining the general health of the school. It would seem to be a question of balance. Balance between, on the one hand, the individual (student and teacher) and the institution and, on the other, development (dealing with change) and maintenance (dealing with the everyday running of the school).

According to the diagram, if the two dimensions are interrelated, organisational health is achieved when:

(i)   all four quadrants of the diagram are not only recognized (in terms of their importance) but also continuously nurtured;
(ii) no imbalances (between the quadrants) are allowed to occur. A school that stresses only one area of activity to the exclusion of the others could be said to be unbalanced and, therefore, unhealthy.

Figure 7.2   The four quadrants

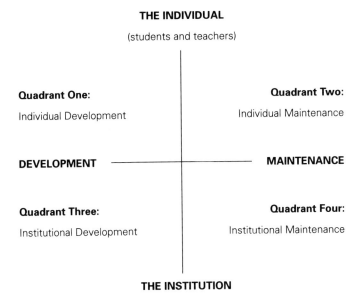

THE INDIVIDUAL

(students and teachers)

Quadrant One: Individual Development	Quadrant Two: Individual Maintenance
DEVELOPMENT ─────────┼───────── **MAINTENANCE**	
Quadrant Three: Institutional Development	Quadrant Four: Institutional Maintenance

THE INSTITUTION

Quadrant One: Individual Development

This quadrant is concerned with the learning, development and growth of individual members of the school — students and teachers alike.

1.1 The Student Dimension

1.1.1   Students first. From what I saw of the classroom experience students generally are having a good deal at Pewton. They receive good teaching and are encouraged to do good learning. According to one student about her teacher, 'He explains it well and makes up good sheets'.

The style of teaching that I witnessed was one I would describe as 'enthusiastic traditional' (which, research says, is often the most favoured style with students and their parents). A mixture of teacher talk — introduction and explanation — followed by the students working on tasks and/or exercises with the teacher circulating around the room dealing with any problems arising — this was the dominant style that I experienced. In one science lesson, the teacher entertained his class. Funny comments abounded such as 'You can't say fairer than that, can you?'; 'No expense has been spared', as he reached for the one beaker available; and 'I don't just throw these lessons together you know'. These got the pupils involved (he got them out the front and invited some to write on the board); and set them to work on well-constructed task sheets back at their benches. Half-way through the lesson he did an explanatory experiment at the front of the room. As one student remarked. 'He explains things well . . . you get high marks'. The whole lesson was well paced and challenging for the students. He worked them hard. Moreover, although this was only the second occasion that he had met with this group, he was already mastering their first names.

I had the same feelings about a French lesson. The 'whole' (the lesson) was constructed from several parts which were well interlaced. Changes of task and pace were handled with a deft hand and the set 2 class ('they should all pass') — responded well to the teacher's easy — not relaxed — discipline, friendly cajoling and task-based approach:

'Andrew, put a sock in it! Have you finished? Then I'll give you some more to do then — stop nattering!'

'Do you want a hand?', asked the teacher of a quiet girl who was having some difficulty with the task; 'Got it? Good!'

'A good, **balanced** lesson', I noted in my commentary. I continued: 'This is a school which clearly achieves good academic results and it cares'.

1.1.2   What I would call 'pastoral teaching' would seem to be the norm, with praise and positive reinforcement as plentiful as reprimands. What is also impressive is that the classroom reality would seem to match the school's rhetoric — its ethos. Books were marked and returned; appropriate homework was set; completed homework was collected — and all with a minimum of fuss.

1.1.3   Differentiation (ie. attending to the learning needs of every individual student) will be a theme of the '90s — and this awareness is clearly growing at Pewton. The emphasis on special needs support (including the workshop during the Teacher Education Day on February 21st) is a clear indication that the school is travelling in this direction. Indeed, says the Headteacher, 'we made a very good staff appointment in the special needs area'. There is more provision now for the lower ability levels. Records of Achievement and the new pilot reporting system based on general and subject criteria (an excellent initiative in my opinion) provide further evidence of this attentiveness to individual student needs.

1.2 The Teacher Dimension

1.2.1   On the subject of individual needs — and turning to the teacher dimension — it would seem that appraisal is being introduced in a most conducive fashion. Staff are involved in the process (through the consultation groups — see quadrant three below) and, quite appropriately, the staff are 'easing' themselves into appraisal through the crucial vehicle of classroom observation.

1.2.2   In an attempt to bring together several threads here, I would suggest the following; that, as part of the classroom observation/appraisal activities, staff members look at the diagram below and ask themselves the following questions:

Is there a case for arguing that our teaching style should shift from being enthusiastic and somewhat teacher-centred (A) to being enthusiastic but more student-centred (B)? What would it look like if students were encouraged to take more responsibility for their own learning?

Quadrant Two: Individual Maintenance

This quadrant is concerned with the everyday maintenance of the school's individual members, especially the students. The substance of

Figure 7.3   Teacher styles

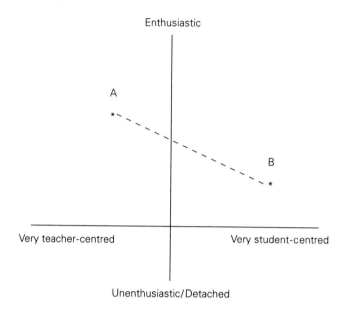

this quadrant, therefore, is pastoral care, counselling and the tutorial system.

2.1   In quadrant one, I have already referred to the quality of the pastoral teaching in the school. There is rich testimony of this from the students:

'One of the good points about the school is that there's always someone you can talk to. There are quite a few nice teachers who are friendly and help you out . . . talk to you in passing and don't talk down to you. They talk to you person to person'.

'It's a small school — you get to know most of the people; nothing bad ever happens — it's quiet really; safe — a good working environment. Everyone's keen to do well — there's not much fooling around'.

'We feel stretched and challenged enough'.

And from a workshop leader (February 21st): 'Parents have commented on the school's persistence and patience with their children'.

2.2 The school clearly cares for the academic, social and emotional well-being of the students. It is significant that staff members requested a counselling skills workshop on February 21st, which provided them with 'a wider reference than only a pastoral slant. Counselling is helping behaviour (throughout the school); being with people and not doing to them'.

2.3 I was struck by the emphasis on individual 'wellness' in the Pewton School community. Both my 'mentor' students are sports-minded and are members of local sports teams. Involvement in PE and sports, is all part of the attention paid to the well-functioning, whole person. Interestingly, one student commented on the 'fierce rivalry' in sports in the middle school: 'It's strange when you come together here. . . . the competition has to be forgotten'.

2.4 Healthy, balanced students do not just happen; they are the product of a great deal of attention and hard work. Indeed, I found the attention to detail impressive. For example, in the staff's morning briefing, attention was drawn to:

- the fact that the Year 13 reports had been in on time — and a big 'thank you' given (in itself a rarity in my experience);
- the arrangements for an upcoming disco;
- the death of a student's mother;
- the sale of sports clothes;
- the agenda for the PACT meeting, etc.

2.5 All this detail is the stuff of a functional, healthy system. Only one dysfunctional element seemed to be present — registration time! With assemblies two days a week and 'tutorial time' on the other three days, the latter is not an unimportant part of the school week. Perspectives on this time differ. Students seem to view it as a 'waste of time'; one of the February workshop leaders remarked that 'registration is not suitable for counselling', while I was told that 'registration time is left open to do counselling.' In addition, of course, records of achievement have to be compiled and career advice given to the students. Given the caring ethos of the school, I am signalling that this would seem to be an issue to be addressed by the staff — probably, yet again!

Quadrant Three: Institutional Development

This quadrant is concerned with change and how the school goes about change. Of some relevance here, therefore, is the school's IDP and the accompanying planning process.

3.1 In interview with the headteacher, she had some interesting insights into change at Pewton:

'A fair bit has changed. I spent the first eighteen months looking — you don't want to spoil things that are good; you don't want to get the staff against you. I wanted to become aware of staff needs — I didn't want to crash about. I wanted to launch into improvements while nurturing the staff; otherwise, change implies criticism'.

'There are some things I just can't do, so I don't want to interfere and spoil them for others. It's essential that I do well the things I'm good at'.

3.2 Talking with other staff, I got a real impression of a school building its own **development culture** (see Holly and Southworth, 1989). This involves a systematic, organic, and developmental approach to change; it's a case of making haste slowly and Pewton seems to have internalized this message:

- 'We're cautious about not jumping too soon'.
- 'We don't jump on all the bandwagons'.
- 'We're good managers of change — there's an avoidance of unnecessary change'.
- 'We're not in the vanguard of change. I guess we're fairly conservative; we're not a pilot for DOVE. There's a great quietness and dignity here'.
- 'Staff are protected from jumping through unnecessary hoops'.
- 'We do the ones (the changes) that are appropriate'.
- 'We don't leap on everything; we're discriminating. We don't want to overburden the staff. We make them aware of what is absolutely necessary . . . We've taken on imposed changes well'.

In 1991 a report was published by the Rand research organisation called 'Schools with Character'. The main thrust of the report was to suggest that a school should establish its educational vision (or ethos) and then should ward off innovation overload by only innovating in order to strengthen the vision, ie, using the vision to filter changes in or out of the school. I see all of this happening at Pewton High School. A balanced healthy institution cannot afford to get totally sucked into quadrant three and the maelstrom of change.

3.3 A good example of this measured and focused approach to change is the Diploma of Vocational Education (DOVE) Working Party:

'We're taking our time about it; we're not going to hurry into it. In Year 10 30% of our students have special needs. We did a pupils questionnaire — which needs further analysis. This is typical of our cautious approach — avoiding headaches. We don't want to give staff any more work than they've already got. We don't want wall-to-wall meetings: the staff appreciate being not unnecessarily overloaded'.

Alternatively, observed another colleague, 'more Young Turks are needed around the place. We could do with a bit more "zip", a bit more challenge'.

3.4 In terms of the processing of change at Pewton, a major innovation has been the establishment of the consultation (or contact) groups. One of the deputy heads takes up the story:

'I returned cautiously from the SHA course.* We wanted to get rid of staff meetings and make better use of the time. Meetings after school are not popular — they seem to go against our culture. As no real agenda appeared, we used the groups as working parties. All staff opted to work on one of several key themes (the environment, communications, equal opportunities, links with industry/community, technology across the curriculum, etc). Now we're creating new groups for processing appraisal . . . it's vital that the staff takes ownership and voices its concerns. There has to be participation

---

* The author of this report, Peter Holly, co-directed this SHA course on School Development Plans in 1989.

in the process, the down-side of which is that we have to meet after school when everyone is tired'.

According to another senior member of staff: 'The consulta-tion groups are about communicating across the staff and about making it (the change agenda) their own . . . It gives staff members a chance to talk about what they want to do about something. Appraisal — they're making it their own; it's very positive. Their attitude is let's take it on board and make it work for us'.

Quadrant Four: Institutional Maintenance

This quadrant is concerned with the school's organisational climate and its impact on the everyday life of the school.

4.1 Undoubtedly, Pewton High School has a well-developed organisational climate which is closely linked to the ethos (or culture) of the school. A key person in creating and main-taining this climate is the headteacher herself:

'I'm a people's head. I think my forte is managing people; creating the environment, the style, the mythology . . . I'm not a systems person — I'm not the type who revels in LMS, an accountant'.

'We're doing all right on the ethos side . . . we're doing pretty nicely . . . The ethos is so important — it's the basis of our culture, our beliefs commonly held. It has to reflect our val-ues, our spiritual beliefs'.

'You have to spell it out — make reference to the aims of the school . . . in assemblies, school council meetings, etc. It was invented for the school prospectus — then we worked back-wards through the consultation groups and revised it in the light of their feedback'.

4.2 What are the elements of Pewton's ethos?, I asked.

'They (the staff) are humane to each other; disabilities are accepted throughout the school. Tolerance. Care for the environment. Mutual care. Warmth'.

'Caring for the environment is really important. So is increasing ownership; sharing the place for a common purpose. This reduces confrontation and aggression — it's more co-operative . . . it's not done to them . . . everybody counts'.

'High standards. There's an implicit contract. The staff make sure homework is done and appropriate and marked work is returned promptly . . . We have to avoid slippage — unconstructive time — like getting late to lessons, nothing going on in registration time, etc.'

4.3 Clearly the clients not only support the ethos (the rhetoric), but see it as a reality. Their support is indicated by the pupil numbers:

'Our number on roll is my achievement', says the head; 're-cruiting pupils has stopped the rot . . . we've got a big, fat sixth form'.

'Parents are happy with the school; performance indicators that they like include:

- the high attendance rate (throughout the school)
- hardly any staff absence
- the staff good at covering (ie. substituting) for each other
- extra-curricular activities
- the school's hospitality
- the excellent examination results
- the school uniform
- the minimal number of exclusions

'These are all general indicators of a school's health'.

'The school really is a little gem — it just needed polishing. They didn't realise what an asset they'd got; it just needed more care'.

Indeed, the client satisfaction mentioned above can best be accounted for in the following chart:

Figure 7.4   Client satisfaction

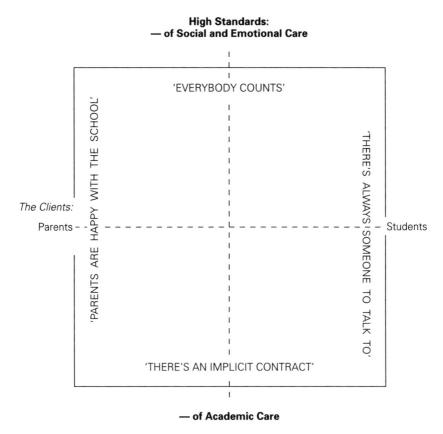

High Standards:
— of Social and Emotional Care

'EVERYBODY COUNTS'

'PARENTS ARE HAPPY WITH THE SCHOOL'

'THERE'S ALWAYS SOMEONE TO TALK TO'

The Clients:

Parents

Students

'THERE'S AN IMPLICIT CONTRACT'

— of Academic Care

Again, it is a question of balance. Parents **and** students alike feel supportive of the school and its efforts — and those efforts hinge on high standards and expectations in terms of both social and emotional care and academic care: the caring school indeed. As evidenced in February's behaviour management workshop, it is neither hard-edged nor soft-edged: it is neither inflexible in terms of its high standards nor over-tolerant in terms of its 'caring-ness'. There is always a fine balance to be struck and this is one school which seems to be getting it right. Ably led by a headteacher who has 'kept the staff together', they are united in the spirit that 'if a job is worth doing, then let's get on and do it'. Pewton High School is truly an example of 'the school that cares'.

Figure 7.5   The basic framework

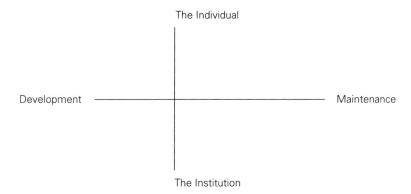

CASE STUDY TWO: 'GENERALLY A BETTER SCHOOL'

This 'portraiture' of Strawford High School has been prepared by Peter Holly for general discussion inside the school as part of its 1992 institutional development planning process. It is based on a framework of four quadrants which are produced by interlinking two dimensions, the individual and the institution and development and maintenance (see below). As much as possible, the actual words of respondents have been included in the text. The idea of a portraiture is to provide a commentary by an external 'critical friend' in order to stimulate internal reflection and dialogue.

Quadrant One

This quadrant is about individual development — of students and teachers alike.

In terms of the 'managed' development and learning progress of individual students, this is where Strawford High School has a 'rare ethos'. 'No one slips through the net . . . no one is unimportant; everyone is supported. Low attaining and middle range students do not get lost in the pack'.

While 'working hard has street-cred here', Strawford is 'certainly not too grammar schoolish'. The head, for one, would refute such a description. The school does have a 'work ethic' built on 'high expectations' and personal success. According to the students, it has a teaching staff of a 'high standard', who can maintain sound discipline and enable their pupils to earn a 'lot better grades': 'They don't push you too hard, but if you're way ahead of the class, they don't just leave you there — they encourage you to do even more'.

It is true, of course, that Strawford exists in a competitive situation. 'A' level results are constantly under 'customer' scrutiny and the school 'can never afford to rest on its laurels'.

In five ways, however, Strawford is supplying a rounded education which caters for the needs of an all-ability student population.

1.1 Courses are being offered in the pre-vocational area (including Business and Information Studies in Year 10 and the new DOVE course(s) which are 'more accessible to those failing 'A' levels'. The current BTEC foundation course, CPVE, work experience, work shadowing, not to mention TVEI, are all examples of the school's desire to cater for a more open 'sixth form'. DOVE would seem to build on CPVE, but 'goes further'; it has 'tightened up' CPVE and leads into the GNVQ, thus filling the 'hole in the middle' and providing substantial opportunities for 'iffy 'A' Level candidates'.

1.2 Every student is 'supported individually by teacher, tutor, head of year and other students'. Mr Rxxx, for instance, organizes the excellent scheme whereby sixth formers give of their own time to offer less able pupils in-classroom support. While there is no 'C' band in the school, 'B' band students are often in need of this more intensive coaching within their curriculum. The worry has been the 'fate of the less able inside the work ethic ethos'; challenges are needed for them too. So Mr Rxxx has taken a 'non-remedial approach to special needs', which incorporates the use of the sixth form students in their curriculum support role. As a result of the sixth formers helping in lessons, the 'less able kids get better attention and their skills are improved — it (the scheme) really helps them to understand'. According to the recipients (a small group of mathematics students with three sixth formers in attention), 'it helps us a lot. We get personal attention. It's more individual — you benefit from it. Encouragement is a very good thing'.

According to the sixth formers involved, 'it makes them think about other people . . . and, in a curious kind of way, helps them to understand more and consolidate their own learning'. According to a staff member, it enables the sixth formers to 'show their leadership skills'.

As Strawford High School hones its attentiveness to the developmental needs of individual students, Mr Rxxx is a 'key member of staff'. 'Behind the middle class gloss, we have the full range of ability including students with limited abilities and with real learning problems'.

Indeed, Mr Rxxx's dual role seems to speak to the essential character of Strawford. On the one hand, he teaches 'A' level English and, on the other, he is responsible for special needs provision. He sees a small number of pupils during registration and assembly but also works (inside and across the curriculum) with subject teachers — constructing appropriate teaching materials — and with the co-ordinators for special needs in each faculty. As **differentiation** (ie. full attention to the differing individual needs of all students) grows in importance, so will Mr Rxxx's role and, indeed, those of other members of staff. Access to the curriculum will become a prime concern with lunch-time sessions (arising from 'worries about the top-end') and the like becoming a more formal part of the mainstream curriculum. Success for all (and the ensuing impact on the self-esteem of every student) lies at the heart of the Strawford vision.

1.3   Attention to individual learning needs (differentiation) demands differentiated means of assessment — thus the growing importance of records of achievement. 'This is not something we've quite got right yet — it started on the pastoral side originally'.

Records of achievement, however, have the potential to 'heal' the pastoral/academic split in that they look to the whole child. At Strawford the use of ROA's is being extended from Year 10 to Year 9 to Year 11 — and then to Year 12 and 13. With the new national record having 'more status in the eyes of the students', presumably its extended use will be a priority at Strawford over the coming months.

1.4   GCSE (and its concomitant attempt to cater for all students) has had a major impact at Strawford. Indeed, it parallels what the school is about — especially **success for all**. Consequently, there are now some questions about how many further changes will have to be introduced in order to bring GCSE in line with the demands of the National Curriculum. There is a move at Strawford to 'retain English coursework', while 'balanced science' in the National Curriculum can 'lead to loss of depth and a superficial coverage of content', and the 'dilution of the three sciences'. Twelve 'periods of science', countered another member of staff, 'represented an unbalanced curriculum and, in any case, new 'A' level modules can be inserted to cover the lost ground'. Undoubtedly, however, GCSE, with its emphasis on 'content **and** process and a range of teaching styles' has been a resounding success at Strawford. Take the English department. Drama improvisations and theatre trips have clearly added to the richness of the students' 'learning experiences'.

1.5   Given the points listed above, Strawford is 'not an exam factory'. Although this may be its popular image (and, maybe, part of its popular appeal, there are currently more takers than places to take them) the school's emphasis is on a 'rounded product'. Besides the tutoring mentioned above, sixth formers are invited to study a full range of core subjects including environmental studies, investigating the arts, modern world affairs, games, information technology and either French or Russian. Extra-curricular activities are in abundance. They not only help to establish 'different relationships' but also 'bring culture into the students' lives'. The impressive Duke of Edinburgh scheme, the Young Enterprise Group, the school magazine, drama workshops, the annual summer ball, Valentine's Day roses, musical evenings and events of all kinds, a Christmas carol service and PTA functions all help to provide an atmosphere in the school which is challenging and caring, robust and rounded. 'It is during extra-curricular activities that good relationships are built up. Staff want to do things for and with the kids. At a recent drama workshop, staff and students were on the floor together. They enjoy working together. Maybe we are not a young staff, lots of new young, energetic blood is needed and that can come from the students!'

The individual development of the teaching staff is very much the territory to be traversed by the school's own teacher appraisal scheme. While it is still early days in the introduction of such a scheme, the cautious and systematic approach being adopted will surely put the school and its staff in good stead when the scheme becomes a reality. The identification of individual training needs and individual development plans (including target-setting) will no doubt be the mainsprings of such a scheme, thus reflecting the kind of student activities being encouraged as part of a more differentiated curriculum provision.

Quadrant Two

This quadrant is about **individual maintenance** — again, of students and teachers alike. In terms of the individual maintenance of the students the focus here is on personal, social and moral education — and the school's pastoral care activities undertaken by form tutors and heads of year are both crucial in this context.

The role of head of year is obviously important, although not 'problem free'. 'Heads of year do everything. We are general dogsbodies. We pick up discipline. Although it is supposed to be dealt with in the classroom (and in the subject areas), it is often quicker just to deal with it yourself. We seem to have lost our status in the school. With only ten 'frees' out of forty, we have more to do what with records of achievement, assemblies, tutorials, etc. We're trying hard with no pats on the back!'

The same teacher was quick to point out the benefits of records of achievement, however: 'They provide a better picture including the interests and sports of the students, and they can be used during job interviews and to accompany work experience and work shadowing'.

While records of achievement have the potential to speak to both the individual development and maintenance of students and their learning, they have to be institutionalized in such a way that their introduction and implementation do not fall on the shoulders of a few members of staff. There has to be joint responsibility and a joint investment.

Again, on the teaching side, counselling skills will be a major component of any good appraisal scheme aimed to promote the individual maintenance of the teaching staff. Can the teachers 'stand the pace of change?', asked one member of staff. They can if 'change' is processed and managed, but this is the focus of quadrant three.

Quadrant Three

This quadrant is about **institutional development**, characterized by the work of the **institutional development plan** (of which this report is a part), which itself is embedded in what Holly and Southworth (1989) have called the '**development culture**'. The latter is not the culture of innovation. It is about systematic growth; change that is planned for and 'packaged for success'. It is about prioritizing and pacing the changes; it is a measured, balanced approach to change. Strawford having flirted briefly with the culture of innovation (and its problems of faddism and overload) would now seem to be settling down to meeting the demands of the development culture. 'Change is now so fast; you have to keep a balance — but how do we do this?'

'When the new bushy-tailed head arrived he had something of a whizz-kid image. After the first flurry (of changes) things have settled. He has eased back a bit'.

'We have to retain 'standards', if there is too much going on, the teaching will suffer, teachers will be too busy to teach'.

'You have to pick the ones (the changes) that affect your school. You have to agree that this is the way we're going and then push the ones you want to push'.

'The head has been a breath of fresh air. He came at the right time; change was inevitable and he had an image of coming with new fangled ideas. (But) he takes criticism; he's open and reflective. He's enthusiastic but guards against too many changes at the same time'.

'It's all about fairly carefully timed initiatives — it's all timing now'.
   Despite this more systematic and focused approach to change, however, staff members voiced the following anxieties:

- an energetic, innovative staff member mentioned her concern about appraisal (as one initiative) having to compete with so many other changes leaving them all under-resourced.
- another colleague mentioned the 'proliferation of meetings, committees and working parties'.
- several staff members described their common concern: that too often, changes are 'initiated but not followed through to their conclusion'. Moreover, it is sometimes the case that 'group recommendations are not acted upon'. Follow-through is a key issue.
- Despite all this activity 'has the classroom changed?' asked another colleague, touching on another crucial issue.

The systematic approach is clearly holding sway, however, as is evidenced in the following comments:

- 'TVEI has been supporting in directions in which we wanted to go — it meant sharing responsibility and leadership (as opposed to being told what to do). It revitalized us'.
- 'Records of achievement are the result of cumulative changes'.
- 'As far as change is concerned, concerning DOVE, we held back . . . we are not a pilot'.
- 'We have put a lot of planning into our Teacher Education Days on appraisal. John Matthias helped us with our interview techniques and, in terms of personal level self-assessment, our counselling and listening skills. The aim was to **support** a staff maybe frightened of appraisal'. 'We didn't want it to be tacked on to everything else; it's not a big push . . . in fact, it's being 'slid' in slowly — staff worries are being elicited'.
- 'Concerning the question of sixth form uniform, lots of people (students) were pushing the rules. The Sixth Form Committee sent a draft to the Headteacher; meetings were then held. It's now a temporary scheme until Easter at which point there will be a review of the pilot'.

Concerning the IDP, there would seem to be two areas of possible confusion:

- is the IDP the sum total of individual training needs or is it something more than that? What is the relationship between these professional development/training needs and institutional development needs? The attempt to link appraisal with the IDP should have a bearing on this discussion;
- which group has the responsibility for drawing up the IDP -the PDG or the CDG? Certainly planning activities seem to be a preoccupation of both groups, but, at the moment, it is the responsibility of the PDG to plan and organize the Teacher Education Days, while the CDG seems to be responsible for the kind of deliberation normally associated with working on an IDP:

   'A list was drawn up at the beginning of the year and then prioritized. One of the priorities that emerged was reporting in Year Nine, according to the stipulations of

the National Curriculum. An offshoot priority was pupil
involvement in their own assessment (and there are now
pilots in each faculty). CDG seems to be taking charge
(of planning) more, but it is always up to each faculty
how they'll do it. It's a question of gaining the commitment of all, then leaving it open. In science, for
instance, year nine topic reviews/student self-assessment
are being piloted, while in mathematics coursework reviews are currently under scrutiny. All the ideas will be
brought together after Easter then documented for the
staff'.

Clearly there are issues to be addressed concerning the IDP process
generally and its role within the school at large.

Quadrant Four

This quadrant is about **institutional maintenance**. Central to the
activities in this quadrant is the role of Strawford's **organizational
culture** which holds together the institution and keeps it on an even
keel. 'This is a small, happy school . . . (while) every member of
staff has a bundle of roles, especially given their investment in extra-
curricular activities, there are many compensations. There's the ethos,
the feeling of being a family, the good relationships and the work
ethic (both mentioned above), the fact that pupils are not teased or
bullied when they want to do well, and the comparative lack of
indiscipline'.

One individual student mentioned that she 'chose to come
here . . . it was a positive move on my part because of the school's
good reputation. There's better behaviour here, it's **generally a better
school** . . . There's a nice atmosphere and a good level of attention'.
Another student talked of the fact that his 'parents moved to the locality to get in the system'. While sometimes feeling a 'bit sheltered' (he
does not feel exposed to the 'hard facts of life') he is appreciative that
the 'school village is safe and secure'. The fact that this same student
is keen to be head-boy denotes that he has bought into the school's
values. Sporting opportunities, school productions and a wealth of
musical offerings all add to the tone of the school. It can be argued,
therefore, that the school has a strong, cohesive organizational culture
which is appealing to students, teachers and parents alike.

Aside from cultural considerations, however, organizationally speaking, the school seems less sure-footed. There is clearly some overlap and confusion of responsibility between the various leading groups in the school, the PDG, the CDG and the HAB (as first evidenced in Quadrant Three). Each group is presently causing some concern:

'The Curriculum Development Group (CDG) meets nine times a year. It now consists of heads of faculty and a few others, although it started out as 'interested parties.' Communication is the concern. Heads of faculty have their own agendas and anything outside these agendas doesn't get passed on. Communication only happens if it's important to them. CDG and PDG used to report back at staff meetings — but they were dropped in order to be more active'.

'PDG is becoming the hand-maiden to the CDG but there's a communication gap'.

'The Professional Development Group (PDG) is suffering from a lack of clarity and lack of co-ordination. Is it responsible for drawing up the IDP? There's not enough cross-fertilization and too much duplication. It's also a question of timing -synchronizing the curriculum and INSET responses'.

'(Responsibility for) appraisal has been given to CDG and HAB. . . . PDG is not quite the body to run the IDP or appraisal'.

'The Head's Advisory Board (HAB) was used originally as a sounding-board and for rubber-stamping decisions — CDG and PDG were workforces reporting to it. Does it need to be reconstituted and used for policy-making?'

'There's a need for one **development group** — the system breaks down and there's a need to oversee this'.

Besides these three over-lapping groups, the head and his deputies have weekly time-tabled meetings. Their meetings are seen as one piece of evidence that the school is 'still hierarchical — but at least now we're got an input'. The management style of the senior staff team is of some interest here. 'I have no concept of what the senior staff do, but I appreciate their approachability'.

Indeed, since the arrival of the new head, there has been 'more management . . . more of a hierarchy', yet 'more participation'. It is perfectly consistent to be participative and more hierarchical. Indeed, says the head, in terms of a 'management structure — we've gone from nil to now'.

It is true to say that some staff feel comfortable with these changes and some staff do not. It is also true that LMS can add to the perceptions that 'management' is on the increase. In a very real sense, it is. At Strawford at least one senior position is almost totally tied down by 'administration' (including capitation; the calendar; health and safety, duty rosters; insurance; buildings, furniture and fabric; lettings; school grounds; stock control; cleaning; security; statistical information; staff bulletin and handbook).

What is clear from this description of the activities of quadrant four is that there is a job to be done. The important management groups in the school have to be sorted out and rationalized. One development group has been suggested (see above). Moreover, the concerns of the heads of year have to be considered in this same discussion. Possibly two major groups are required, one for development and one for maintenance. The one group could oversee and co-ordinate the activities of quadrants one and three and the other group quadrants two and four. Much discussion is needed around these tentative suggestions. One possibility, of course, is that with all the recent emphasis on change and development, the maintenance side has been somewhat under-played. Certainly, a healthy organization tries to keep a balanced approach to the four quadrants.

Hopefully, by talking to teachers and students and observing the school at work, an authentic picture of Strawford has been drawn in this report. According to the head: 'I've been here four years as head and my arrival was simultaneous with the explosion of change . . . I feel we have a rare ethos, but am I too easily convinced with my own propaganda?!'

Certainly, there will be a continuing need to ask two central questions:

- in each of the quadrants described above, what is the rhetoric and what is the daily reality?
- and, as one teacher asked, have all the changes had any real impact on the classroom level?

When a school receives and acts upon a portraiture it is going a long way towards becoming a Learning School (see Holly and Southworth,

Figure 7.6   The classroom inventory

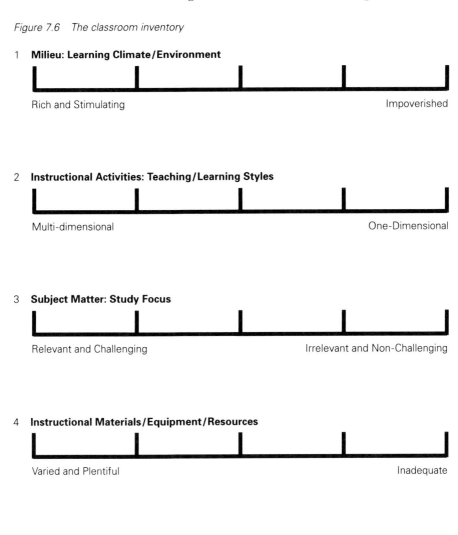

1   **Milieu: Learning Climate/Environment**

Rich and Stimulating   Impoverished

2   **Instructional Activities: Teaching/Learning Styles**

Multi-dimensional   One-Dimensional

3   **Subject Matter: Study Focus**

Relevant and Challenging   Irrelevant and Non-Challenging

4   **Instructional Materials/Equipment/Resources**

Varied and Plentiful   Inadequate

5   **Involvement**

Deep/Totally Engaged   Dis-engaged and Dis-interested

Colin Bayne-Jardine and Peter Holly

Figure 7.6   (Cont'd)

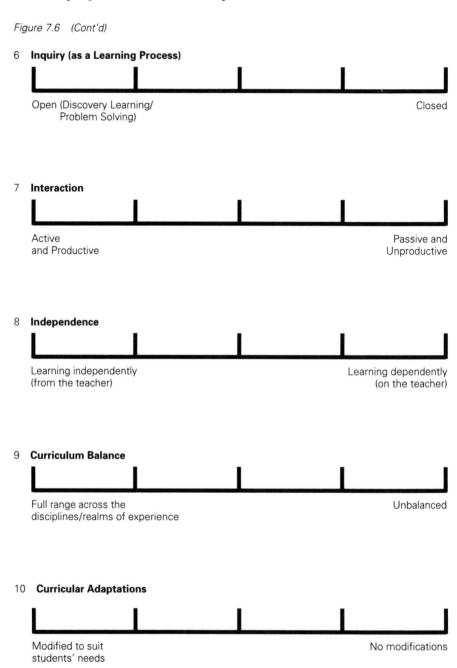

6 **Inquiry (as a Learning Process)**

Open (Discovery Learning/   Closed
Problem Solving)

7 **Interaction**

Active   Passive and
and Productive   Unproductive

8 **Independence**

Learning independently   Learning dependently
(from the teacher)   (on the teacher)

9 **Curriculum Balance**

Full range across the   Unbalanced
disciplines/realms of experience

10 **Curricular Adaptations**

Modified to suit   No modifications
students' needs

Figure 7.6   (Cont'd)

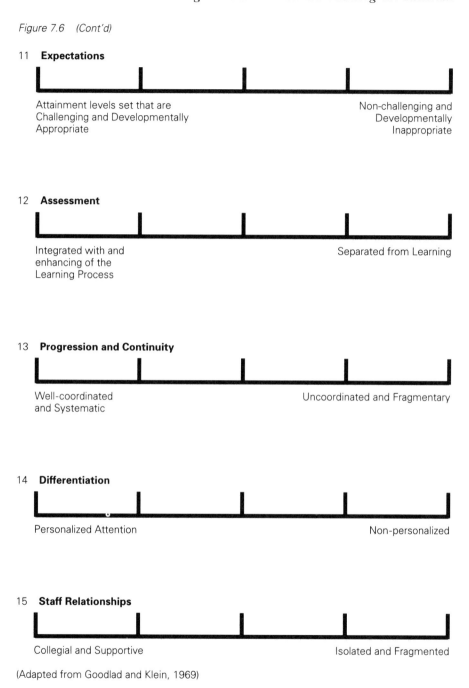

11   Expectations

Attainment levels set that are
Challenging and Developmentally
Appropriate

Non-challenging and
Developmentally
Inappropriate

12   Assessment

Integrated with and
enhancing of the
Learning Process

Separated from Learning

13   Progression and Continuity

Well-coordinated
and Systematic

Uncoordinated and Fragmentary

14   Differentiation

Personalized Attention

Non-personalized

15   Staff Relationships

Collegial and Supportive

Isolated and Fragmented

(Adapted from Goodlad and Klein, 1969)

1989). It is internalizing the external. By then following up this experience with sustained peer observation using a technique such as the classroom inventory (see above) it is creating a learning culture within itself. Moreover, action research (which revolves around such techniques as portraiture and the classroom inventory) is central to the growth of such a culture. Action research leads to changes and, indeed, changes the way we go about change. Holly (1992) has argued that effective change involves a dualistic approach. Change agents need to be:

- more determined yet more discerning;
- more enthusiastic yet more evaluative;
- more skilled yet more sceptical;
- more planning-conscious yet more playful/opportunistic.

Action research, of course, not only embraces these dualisms, it is dualistic itself. It is research-driven action for change. It is action-driven research. It is the two sides of learning.

8   Striving for Congruence:
The Properties of a Learning System

Peter Holly

A learning system is composed of interdependent parts. It is a system in which the 'parts' are able to act both independently and dependently. The 'dependency' tends to come from the over-arching culture (thus providing for systemic convergence), while the 'independency' rests in the ability of the 'parts' to be divergent in thought and deed — while remaining within a framework of core values pertaining to learning itself. A learning system, echoing Karl Weick, Peters and Waterman (1982) and Handy (1989) has simultaneous loose-tight properties. There has to be systemic congruence (see Holly, 1991) but not totalitarianism. Mutuality, reciprocity, responsiveness and co-operation are matched by flexibility, dynamism, openness and challenge. Throughout the system it is a case of collaborative individualism. The system parts have to show initiative and be self-standing and be capable of joining together to provide integrity. Indeed, Beckhard and Pritchard argue that a learning organization (the equivalent of a system 'part') has two major characteristics: it encourages innovation and it approaches problems in an integrative way. Kanter (1983) reminds us that the latter, the ability 'to see the whole as opposed to parts and to challenge the established patterns rather than walling off a piece of experience', is a vital characteristic of a changing and learning organization. In similar vein, Senge emphasizes the power of metanoia — the capacity to act systematically and thus release the full potential of synergism.

Senge refers to this capacity as the fifth discipline. The others, he says, are personal mastery, changing our mental models, building shared visions and team learning/dialogue. But it is systems thinking, the fifth discipline, that creates the holistic, integrative power possessed by a learning system. Any learning system or learning organization has to

Peter Holly

Figure 8.1   *The learning system: collaborative inquiry*

Congruence System-Wide

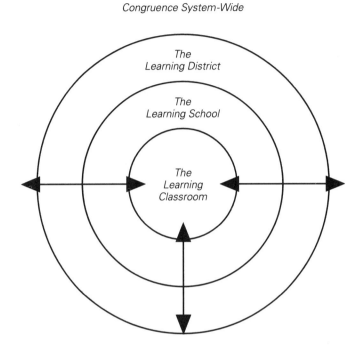

have a system for learning and, therefore, a system for changing. As Holly and Southworth contend in terms of the Developing School, it is a learning organization that is organized for learning. Such a school is constantly self-evaluating its own performance; it is constantly speaking to itself and receiving feedback. This formative, process evaluation work (which often takes the form of action research) provides on-going information for staff decision-making concerning change planning and replanning. It is an interactive process of needs assessment which enables a learning school to systematically improve the learning of its students. This is what Holly (1992) refers to as the 'package deal' for school-based development: action research for informed and participative decision-making for effective change management — in the interests of student learning (see chapter one).

System-wide congruence comes when the different levels of the system are singing to the same tune, albeit in counterpoint, when they apply reciprocally the principles of action research/collaborative inquiry and learning itself.

Establishing a Learning System at the Local Level

Our recommendations are grounded in the belief that reform is most needed where learning takes place — in the individual schools, in the classroom, and in the interaction between teacher and student. As businessmen world-wide have learned, problems can best be solved at the lowest level of operation. While structures are needed, bureaucracies tend to focus on rules and regulations rather than results, thus stifling initiative. Therefore, we believe that school governance should be retained at the local level, and not be supplanted by statewide boards of education or national dictates. However, states should set standards and provide the guidance and support to local schools that are necessary for meeting these standards.

If, as Timar and Kirp (1987) have argued above, locally-based/site-based development constitutes a new way of generating change in education and a new change theory, then other 'theories' (organisation theory, management theory and, above all evaluation theory) have to follow suit. And, as Charles Handy (1989) has argued, they all have much to learn from learning theory. Indeed, it has been argued that the 'system' has been designed to respond to change from the top, but that when those who are locally-based teachers, principals and local administrators initiate change and create new knowledge, the larger 'system' doesn't know how to respond. Much of the old 'dogma' is palpably out-dated. According to Sirotnik (1989):

Perhaps the most insidious of these dogmas is the presumed split between research and practice that John Dewey spent a lifetime trying to repair. The damage is still with us, and it becomes particularly apparent when the dominant view of educational change and school improvement — R, D, D, and E — is critically appraised. This linear model of 'research, development, diffusion, and evaluation' essentially puts experts against practitioners. Those 'in the know' are the scholars that generate the research and the experts that package and disseminate the findings in usable form and evaluate the use of these packages in practice. Those 'in need of knowing' are the practitioners, the workers in schools, the consumers of new knowledge once it is appropriately distilled in inservice programs. School-based educators are seen as deficient in one or more skill areas and in need of retraining, rather than as professionals

Figure 8.2   Control of action research

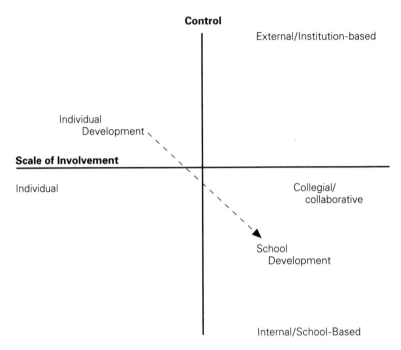

who reflect upon their work and upon ways in which they might do their work better. Schools are seen as places in disrepair and in need of fixing, rather than as messy social systems in the process of evolution.

Changing schools, then, becomes a process of programmatic intervention and installation — of applying the remedies of research to the ills of practice. The school is an object to be changed, not a centre of change — developing knowledge and informing agendas of action happen somewhere else (in research universities, R & D centers, and district offices, for example), not as an ongoing part of professional life in schools.

According to the new paradigm, however, the teachers and those close to the practice are the experts — the reflective practitioners, the professionals. They are the ones 'in the know'; their schools are the centres of change. Peter Holly (1988) has noted that action research has travelled from being conducted by individual teachers but under the control of the universities to being conducted as part of more collegial, school-based endeavours controlled by the schools themselves (Figure 8.2)

In addition, J Myron Atkin (1989) has observed that teachers are increasingly 'playing a larger role in systematic inquiry directed towards educational improvement'. Interestingly, in the passage quoted below, he argues that the teacher unions and associations should take the lead in advancing new research policies and practices and thus help in magnifying the role of teachers as researchers and professionals.

Research in the Service of Reform

Regardless of the salience of this particular form of teacher-conducted research, the current scene in education reform seems conducive to teachers' playing a larger role in systematic inquiry directed toward educational improvement. The hurdles are high, however. First, research must come to be seen as an important responsibility in the teaching profession. Then time must be earmarked for the activity. Not least, settings must be created wherein teachers can regularly and easily exchange ideas.

As severe an obstacle as any in the path of significant teacher involvement in research is the dominant culture of the research enterprise, which assigns responsibilities for research to university professors or to specially constituted agencies that undertake analysis on a contract basis. However, as long as academic expectations take priority — and as long as they place the highest value on the generation of theory rather than on the amelioration of practical problems — action research and its close relatives, with their reliance on the perspectives of people inside elementary and secondary schools, are unlikely to thrive.

A more likely prospect for magnifying the role of teachers in research is for the profession itself — the unions and the subject-area organizations — to take the lead in advancing new research policies and practices. Such initiatives may indeed be launched in earnest if the realization grows among teacher leaders that not only do existing patterns of educational research miss many of the most important issues and understandings, but they also do not match the reform ethos that is otherwise spreading across the country.

As in so many aspects of education policy, it is a matter of balance. For educational research to catch up with education reform, more of the responsibility for research must come under the influence of the teachers themselves. Not all of it, of course, but more of it. Collaborative work within someone else's frame of reference can certainly be broadening and useful to teachers and school administrators. Independent work by professors can also be enlightening; the country needs scholarly insights that are not coupled tightly to pressing current problems. But if these are the only kinds of systematic inquiry that receive serious attention within the profession of teaching, the long-term outlook for the initiative and independence of the profession and for our understanding of how schools can be improved is bleak.

The public and the policy community are slowly coming to understand that high-quality teaching is hard to obtain without giving teachers greater independence. Perhaps they will soon come to realize that substantive and continuing educational improvement will be difficult to achieve unless teachers begin to play a greater role in identifying the key impediments to progress in education and in figuring out how to do something about them. The progress of meaningful school reform will be stalled until teachers emerge from their marginal positions in the research community and become full partners in the conception and the conduct of educational inquiry.

As Sirotnik, Myron Atkin and Holly have all pointed out, action research/collaborative inquiry gives more control to the professionals in the situation. It is about professional empowerment. As Kallick (1991) has observed, it gives teachers a new role — not passive recipient, but active learner. Teachers, she says, can ask: does this 'model' (say of co-operative learning) make sense in my classroom? It is a case of conversing/interacting with the model and not allowing external 'experts' to have the final word with what goes on in the classroom. It's also a case of reversing the usual process and of promoting 'practice into theory' — daily practice informing and impacting abstract theory. Teachers are reflecting and interpreting rather than receiving other people's schemes in their entirety (the 'fidelity' approach). Indeed, it has been argued that the 'teacher-as-recipient' approach constitutes, at best, tinkering with the present system, whereas the more reflective, interpretative, proactive approach leads to restructuring. The latter represents the transition to a radical philosophical and practical re-orientation, which hinges on the learning classroom in the learning school (see Holly and Southworth, 1989).

Referring to one such school, Judith Warren Little (1982) has made the following comments:

In one of . . . the schools, classroom observation is so frequent, so intellectually lively and intense, and so thoroughly integrated into the daily work and so associated with accomplishments for all who participate, that it is difficult to see how the practices could fail to improve teaching.

It is a question of intensity and implosion. It is also a case of restructuring at the heart of the system.

In the new, restructured classroom, therefore, there will be:

* new relationships;
* a new focus on both learning itself and learning how to learn;
* an emphasis on such key skills as reflective practice, shared observation and self-evaluation;
* performance-based assessment which is embedded within everyday practice and which acts as an integral spur to learning and development.

Indeed, this is why action research and new approaches to assessment have so much in common. They are:

* classroom-based and focused on teaching and learning;
* formative and developmental;
* cyclical, organic and needs-related;
* data-based;
* relevant to everyday experience;
* the stuff of learning communities.

On the theme of learning communities, Charles Handy (1989) has discussed the nature of learning organizations: 'The Learning Organization can mean two things; it can mean an organization which learns and/or an organization that encourages learning in its people'.

Such an organization, says Handy, is questioning, thoughtful, solutions-seeking and proactive. Moreover, such an organization understands the importance of co-ownership of the questions to be asked, team-work and chunking (see Peters and Waterman, 1983, and Holly, 1991), the impact that comes from the outside stimulus of mentors, and its own endorsement of its members' personal learning, reflection and self-development.

The Learning Organization: Seven Characteristics

If LEAs and Districts — and their member schools — are to become Learning Organizations they will need to attend to these seven characteristics:

1 Learning Organizations look to their future by looking at their present. They have future-oriented visions of learning, but they also know, as Peter Senge (1990) has pointed out, that visions are nothing without a deep understanding of the forces that must be mastered to move from here to there. The current reality has to be understood and shortcomings registered, thus enabling the learning organization to expand its capacity to create its future. 'Adaptive learning' has to be joined by (and, indeed, superseded) by 'generative learning'. Consequently, Learning Organizations are filled with learning. They root learning in the soil of the organization, thus becoming:

> organizations where people continually expand their capacity to create the results they truly desire, where new and expansive patterns of thinking are nurtured, where collective aspiration is set free, and where people are continually learning how to learn together . . .
>
> It is no longer sufficient to have one person learning for the organization . . . It's just not possible any longer to 'figure it out' from the top, and have everyone else following the orders of the 'grand strategist'. The organizations that will truly excel in the future will be the organizations that discover how to tap people's commitment and capacity to learn at all levels in an organization . . .
>
> Real learning gets to the heart of what it means to be human. Through learning we re-create ourselves. Through learning we become able to do something we never were able to do. Through learning we reperceive the world and our relationship to it. Through learning we extend our capacity to create, to be part of the generative process of life. Peter Senge, 1990

2 Learning Organizations institutionalize reflection-in-action. According to Schon (1983):

> . . . the practitioner allows himself to experience surprise, puzzlement, or confusion in a situation which he finds uncertain or unique. He reflects on the phenomena before him, and on the prior understandings which have been implicit in his behaviour. He carries out an experiment which serves to generate both a new

understanding of the phenomena and a change in the situation.

When someone reflects-in-action, he becomes a researcher in the practice context. He is not dependent on the categories of established theory and technique, but constructs a new theory of the unique case. His inquiry is not limited to a deliberation about means which depends on a prior agreement about ends. He does not keep means and ends separate, but defines them interactively as he frames a problematic situation. He does not separate thinking from doing . . . Because his experimenting is a kind of action, implementation is built into his inquiry.

Reflection-in-action enables us to inquire into the reasoning underlying our behaviour and frees us from the trappings of our defensive routines (our 'skilled incompetence') when faced with the pain and threat posed by learning situations. In addition, says Senge, it allows us to recast traditional planning as learning: '(it is) less important to produce perfect plans than to use planning to accelerate learning institutionally'.

3   Learning Organizations, then, treat planning as learning:

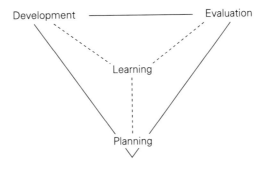

Senge quotes an oil company representative who claims that: 'We think of planning as learning and of corporate planning as institutional learning . . .'

This makes planning more provisional, less certain; more dynamic, less linear; more organic, less mechanistic.

4   Learning Organizations pace their learning and their development:

According to Senge:

> For most American business people the best rate of growth is fast, faster, fastest. Yet, virtually all natural systems, from ecosystems to animals to organizations, have intrinsically optimal rates of growth. The optimal rate is far less than the fastest possible growth. When growth becomes excessive . . . the system will seek to compensate by slowing down; perhaps putting the organization's survival at risk in the process.

Learning Organizations know that learning overload prevents learning as inevitably as learning underload does.

5 Learning Organizations have a 'disciplined' approach, ie they attend to new disciplines. According to Senge:

> We have never approached the subtler tasks of building organizations, of enhancing their capabilities for inno- vation and creativity, of crafting strategy and design- ing policy and structure through assimilating new disciplines.

These disciplines, he says, are the growth of personal mastery on the part of individual staff members, the in-depth investi- gation of mental models, the building of a shared vision, team learning and, the 'governor', systems thinking. All of these have to be hard worn from the inside; it's not a case of 'playing catch up' and trying to emulate the best practice of others.

6 Learning Organizations learn from themselves. External help is required but the temptation to 'fix' an organization from the outside has to be resisted. Says Lewis Thomas (in Senge, 1990):

> When you are dealing with a complex social system . . . with things about it that you are dissatisfied with and eager to fix, you cannot just step in and set about fixing with much hope of helping. The realisation is one of the sore discouragements of our century.

As John Dewey always argued, learning has to be a process of self-discovery. And we must each be our own discoverer;

others cannot do it for us. We must also discover how our efforts are often self-defeating and, when we are self-reliant and self-determining, we have to learn not to blame others for our own shortcomings. When solutions are handed down to us, much of the accountability for success lies with those who came up with the solutions. When we make our own solutions to our own problems, however, much of the accountability lies with us. There's no-one to hold responsible but ourselves. Moreover, Senge argues, people learn most rapidly when they have a genuine sense of responsibility for their actions. If we know, he says, that our fate lies in our own hands, then 'our learning matters'.

> At the heart of a learning organization is a shift of mind — from seeing ourselves as separate from the world to connected to the world, from seeing problems as caused by someone or something 'out there' to seeing how our own actions create the problems we experience. A learning organization is a place where people are continually discovering how they create their reality.

The need to investigate the current reality and to launch into rebuilding programs is internalised, not externalised. Internalisation is a key concept in the Learning Organization. And this is why, says Senge, that learning organizations will, increasingly, be 'localized' organizations.

7 Learning Organizations, like their members, are life-long learners. They 'travel hopefully' on the process of learning. According to Senge:

> To practice a discipline is to be a lifelong learner. You 'never arrive'; you spend your life mastering disciplines. You can never say, 'we are a learning organization', any more than you can say, 'I am an enlightened person'. The more you learn, the more acutely aware you become of your ignorance. Thus, a corporation cannot be 'excellent' in the sense of having arrived at a permanent excellence; it is always in the state of practising the disciplines of learning . . . as the five component learning disciplines converge they will not

create the learning organization but rather a new wave of experimentation and advancement.

And this new wave of experimentation and advancement will lead to a new wave of learning. As Weick (1985) has pointed out, 'managing' this learning process:

> may be more like surfing on waves of events and decisions . . . People who surf do not command the waves to appear, or to have a particular spacing, or to be of a special height. Indeed, surfers do their best with what they get. They can control inputs to the process, but they can't control outcomes. To ride a wave as if one were in control is to act and have faith. The message of newer perspectives often boils down to that.

Charles Handy would agree:

> Those who are always learning are those who can ride the waves of change and who see a changing world as full of opportunities not damages . . . They are also the enthusiasts and the architects of new ways and forms and ideas . . . Unless we take a view we shall be a mere flotsam on the waves of life.

It is a case of learning to ride the waves of learning. We can all be surfers. We can all be hopeful yet informed travellers. We can all be experiential learners. We learn in experience; we reflect on and evaluate our practice, changing course accordingly. Evaluation is our guide and mentor.

The Learning Lab Initiative of the National Education Association (NEA): School District Restructuring

When NEA launched its Learning Labs initiative in the USA in 1988 there was little mention of evaluation. There was much talk — and quite rightly so — about school restructuring, the democratization of public education and the development of the intrinsic power of human beings. It was acknowledged that the central task of the Labs was to re-shape life in the classroom and thus impact at the level of practice.

The aim was to redesign student learning through the introduction of diverse instruction methods tailored to the needs of individual learners and more opportunities for all students to experience active learning, problem-solving, critical thinking and co-operative learning. School staffs, it was said, would be entrusted with the direction to shape what happens in classrooms through the exercise of their professional discretion — thus making them both responsible and accountable for organising student learning opportunities — and would be encouraged to enter into collaborative dialogue in order to foster exchanges of experiences. What was crucially acknowledged was that, while the 'process (of change) is different at each school site', 'top-down reform mandates have too little positive, and often negative, impact on essential conditions of learning . . . real and fundamental change in schooling must emerge from the school site rather than imposed externally or unilaterally'. School-based development (see Holly and Southworth, 1989) was the chosen path to achieving local/site-based restructuring.

The following passage said it all:

> Restructuring cannot be defined by a single, simple definition. It is not a particular curriculum, program, or teaching style, nor the adoption of specific standards, nor the imposition of a distinctive staffing pattern. Because the potential for human learning is unlimited and understanding about learning continues to grow, the restructured school encourages continuing examination of the core elements of schooling-teaching, learning, curriculum, and the interaction of these elements to create a school culture. The restructured school is not stifled by rigid and traditional assembly-line teaching methods and rigid hierarchical administrative school structures that inhibit flexibility and suppress the discovery of fresh ways of thinking and acting.
>
> Restructuring will be achieved when schools have the capacity to try new ways of delivering instruction and new strategies to remove the barriers to learning. The NEA goal is to establish a self-renewing system within which continuous innovation and growth can occur and learning can flourish.
>
> To demonstrate how its vision can be fulfilled, the NEA has launched a Learning Laboratories Initiative to encourage experimentation at the school district level to achieve restructured schools. (NEA, 1988)

The continuing examination of the core elements of schooling (including, vitally, school culture), the discovery of fresh ways of thinking and acting, the establishment of a self-renewing system — all of this is the stuff of the self-developing, self-reviewing, self-evaluating school. But school-based development, as Holly and Southworth have recognised, is not only a new paradigm for schooling, but also a new change paradigm for schools which demands new approaches to evaluation. Moreover, it is no longer tenable to evaluate change in education using the old evaluation approach. While systemic congruence (see Holly, 1990) gives integrity to the package deal, systemic in-congruence is undermining, dysfunctional and leads to fragmentation.

Moreover, when changes are externally generated and imposed on schools (as has been, traditionally, the case), a matching, congruent evaluation is comparatively straight-forward. It is a question of asking:

- has the change been adopted effectively, ie. in its entirety?
- has it been 'installed' in the school?

Ernest House (1981) has referred to this so-called 'fidelity' approach as the technological perspective. Above all, this perspective on evaluation keeps faith with the essence of the change approach which it is intended to support. If school-based development constitutes a new approach to change in schools, therefore, it deserves an evaluation perspective which matches it — and, indeed, enhances it — in both philosophical and practical terms. This 'match' may be provided by the use of collaborative inquiry — which contains a large measure of self-evaluation (see Figure 8.3). Indeed, it can be argued that the power of school-based development as a comprehensive school improvement process is diminished if the act of evaluation/assessment proceeds separately and incongruently. (See chapter four).

In August 1990 Peter Holly threw down the gauntlet to Learning Lab representatives. Essentially, he said, the task was to 'fill in the box' (see below); to create new forms of evaluation congruent with, and supportive of, the new change paradigm in schools and school districts. Learning Labs were charged with the task of learning how to use evaluation to enhance learning-student learning, teacher learning and organizational learning (see Senge, 1990). It is a question, therefore, of not only restructuring and reframing the local school system and the ways in which it goes about renewing itself, but also reconfiguring the relationship between school-based development and evaluation. Building on the work of Donald Schon and Peter Senge, Holly (1990) argued that such a rapprochement should lead to the establishment of a genuine learning system at the local level, a genuine spirit of inquiry, with the school as the centre of inquiry (see Schaefer, 1967) and, therefore, as the centre of change (Sirotnik, 1989).

Figure 8.3   Collaborative inquiry

	Change Perspective	Evaluation Perspective
Former Paradigm	— Externalisation — Interventionist	Technological
Emerging Paradigm	— Internalisation — Intra-Ventionist/ School-Based Development	Collaborative Inquiry

The System that Learns

Throughout this book we have emphasised the centrality of the spirit of inquiry within organisational development — at school and LEA/ school district level. We have arranged our material around the framework of the Six Cs. Building a clear focus and a compelling agenda, educators conduct team-based collaborative inquiry within a culture of development, supported by critical friends, thus creating congruence system-wide. All this adds up to a seventh C, a true community of learners.

And this learning community has a central task — the development of quality schools. Such schools have quality processes that lead to quality products. In the language of Total Quality Management, they concentrate on the process of continuous improvement including constant formative and informative feedback, ie. organizational learning, in order to create the essential product of high quality student learning.

It is interesting to record that the TVEI team (represented in chapter five) are now focusing their efforts on the individual development of student learning — according to the conceptual map offered (Figure 8.4). This map embodies the 6 Cs that we have explored in this present volume. It is the kind of map that makes for a system of learning and helps all involved to continue 'to travel hopefully'.

Peter Holly

Figure 8.4   *A summary of support offered on approaches to learning*

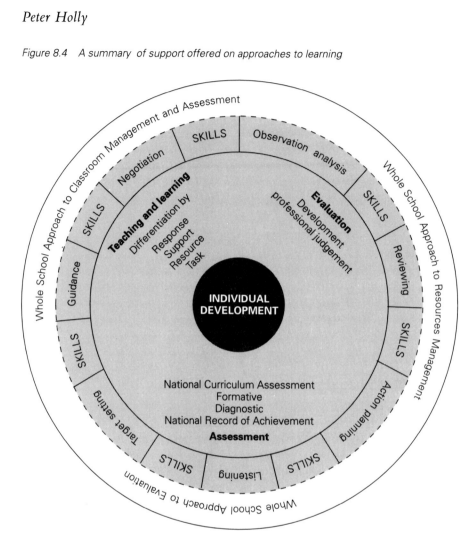

Bibliography

ARGYRIS, C. and SCHON, D.A. (1978) *Organisational Learning: A Theory of Action Perspective*, Reading, MA., Addison-Wesley.

ATKIN, M. (1989) quoted in HOLLY, P.J. (1992) *The X,Y,Z of School-based Evaluation. A Discussion Paper*, Washington, DC, NEA.

BAWDEN, R. (1989) Action research. Conference paper, Brisbane.

BAYNE-JARDINE, C.C. (1991) *The Education Inspectorate*, Hereford and Worcester LEA.

BECKHARD, R. and PRITCHARD, N. (1992) *Changing the Essence: The Art of Creating and Leading Fundamental Change in Organisations*, San Francisco, Jossey-Bass.

BLACKMAN, S. (1987) 'The labour market in school' in BROWN, P. and ASHTON, D. *Education, Unemployment and Labour Markets*, London, Falmer Press.

BRIGHOUSE, T. (1991) *What Makes a Successful school?* Network Press.

BUSH, T. (1989) *Managing Education; Theory and Practice*, Milton Keynes, Open University Press.

DRUMMOND, M.J. (1986) New approaches to teaching and learning. Conference paper, Cambridge Institute of Education.

EISNER, E.W. (1985) *The Art of Educational Evaluation*, London, Falmer Press.

FIDDY, R. and STRONACH, I. (1987) *How Can Evaluation Become Formative?* CARE, University of East Anglia.

FULLAN, M. (1982) *The Meaning of Educational Change*, New York, Teachers College Press.

GUSKEY, T. (1990) (1986) 'Staff development and the process of teacher change', *Educational Researcher*, **15**, 5, pp. 5–12.

HANDY, C.B. (1982) *Understanding Organisations*, London, Penguin Books.

HANDY, C.B. (1989) *The Age of Unreason*, London, Business Books.

HANDY, C.B. (1989) 'By way of encouragement: The path to a better society', *RSA Journal*, **CXXXVI**, 5377.

HARGREAVES, D. (1989) *Planning for School Development*, HMSO.

HARLAND, J. (1987) 'The TVEI experience', in GLEESON, D. *TVEI and Secondary Education*, Milton Keynes, Open University Press.

HOLLY, P.J. (1984) 'The institutionalisation of action research in schools', *Cambridge Journal Of Education*, **14**, 2.

HOLLY, P.J. (1986) 'Teaching for learning, learning for teaching', *Curriculum*, 8.

HOLLY, P.J. (1989) 'Action research: Cul de sac or turnpike?' in KYLE, D.W. and HOVDA, R.A. (Issue Editors) The potential and practice of action research, parts 1 and 2, *Peabody Journal of Education*, **64**, 3.

HOLLY, P.J. (1990) School-based development in action. Schools for the twenty-first century, State of Washington, USA.

HOLLY, P.J. (1991a) 'Action research: The missing link in the creation of schools as centres of inquiry', in LIEBERMAN, A. and MILLER, L. (Eds) *Staff Development*, New York, Teachers College Press.

HOLLY, P.J. (1991b) Action research in twenty-first century schools. Report to the State of Washington.

HOLLY, P.J. (1992) The X,Y,Z of school-based evaluation: A discussion paper, Washington, DC: NEA.

HOLLY, P.J. and ANDERSON, J. (1991) 'Schools for the Twenty-first century', O.S.P.I. Discussion paper, State of Washington.

HOLLY, P.J. and HOPKINS, D. (1988) 'Evaluation and school improvement', *Cambridge Journal of Education*, **18**, 2.

HOLLY, P.J. and SOUTHWORTH, G.W. (1989) *The Developing School*, London, Falmer Press.

HOPKINS, D. (1988) *Doing School-based Review*, Leuven ACCO, University of East Anglia.

HOPKINS, D. (1989) *Evaluation for School Development*, Milton Keynes, Open University.

HOUSE, E. (1981) 'Three perspectives of innovation', in LEHMING, R. and KANE, M. (Eds) Improving Schools: Using What We Know, Beverly Hills, Sage.

KALLICK, B. (1991) Speech at Gheens Professional Development Academy, June Workshop.

KANTER, R.M. (1983) *The Change Masters*, New York, Simon and Schuster.

LEWIS, I. and MUNN, P. (1989) *So You Want to do Research! A Guide for Teachers on How to Formulate Research Questions*, Edinburgh, Scottish Council for Research in Education.

LIGHTFOOT, S.L. (1983) *The Good High School: Potraits of Character and Culture*, New York, Basic Books.

LITTLE, J. (1982) 'Norms of Collegiately as Experimentation', Workplace conditions of school success, *American Ed Research Journal*, **19**, 3, pp. 325–40.

MCMULLAN, I. (1970) 'The clarification of aims and objects as an aid to making decisions', in TAYLOR, P. *The Teacher as Manager*, London, NCET.

NTI (1981) *A New Training Initiative: An Agenda for Action*, London, HMSO.

PETERS, T.J. and WATERMAN, R.H. (1982) *In Search of Excellence*, New York, Harper and Row.

PETERS, T.J. (1989) *Thriving in Chaos*, London, Pan Books.

PLOWDEN REPORT (1967) *Children and their Primary Schools*, London, HMSO.

RUDDUCK, J. (1991) *Innovation and Change: Developing Involvement and Understanding*, Milton Keynes, Open University Press.

RUTTER, M., MAUGHAN, B., MORTIMORE, P. and OUSTON, J. (1979) *Fifteen Thousand Hours: Secondary Schools and their Effects on Children*, London, Open Books.

SAGOR, R. and (1991) *Introduction to Project LEARN*, Washington State University.

SAGOR, R. and HOLLY, P.J. (1990) Workshop introduction, Washington State University.

SCHAEFER, R. (1967) *The School as a Center of Inquiry*, New York, Harper and Row.

SCHON, D.A. (1987) *Educating the Reflective Practitioner*, San Francisco, Jossey Bass.

SENGE, P.M. (1990) *The Fifth Discipline: The Art and Practice of the Learning Organisation*, New York, Doubleday.

SHUMSKY, (1958) 'The personal significance of action research', *Journal of Teacher Education*, **9**, pp. 152–55.

SIROTNIK, K.A. (1989) 'The school as a center of change', in SERGIOVANNI, J.J. and MOORE, J.H. (Eds) *Schooling for Tomorrow: Directing Reforms to Issues that Count*, Boston, Allyn and Bacon.

SIZER, T.R. (1984) *Horace's Compromise: The Dilemma of the American High School*, Boston, Houghton-Mifflin.

TIMAR, T.B. and KIRP, D.L. (1987) 'Educational reform and institutional competence', *Harvard Educational Review*, **57**, 3, pp. 308–30.

TYERMAN, M. (1968) *Truancy*, London, University of London Press.

WEICK (1985) 'Sources of order in underorganized systems: Themes in recent organizational theory', in LINCOLN, Y.S. (Ed.) Organizational

Theory and Inquiry: The Paradigm Revolution, Beverly Hills, CA, Sage.

WHITEHEAD, A.N. (1932) *The Aims of Education*, London, Benn.

WILLIAMS (1991) In conversation with the author. Puget Sound Educational Consortium.

Biographical Notes

Colin Bayne-Jardine Went to Hereford and Worcester as Principal County Inspector in 1988 from Staffordshire where he was senior secondary inspector. Before joining the Staffordshire Inspectorate he had been Head of Henbury School, Bristol, and before that head of a reorganized comprehensive school in Bath. Teaching experience has been in independent schools, comprehensive schools and in Canada and the USA. He has written history textbooks and contributed to a number of educational books on management and the curriculum.

Tim Brighouse has been a teacher of people of all ages. He was for more than a decade a Chief Education Officer and has worked in the North, the Midlands, London and Wales. He has visited thousands of schools. He was Research Machines Professor of Education at the University of Keele and the Director of a Centre conducting a research project into successful schooling and is now Chief Education Officer, Birmingham.

Denis Gleeson in Professor of Education and Director of the Centre for Social Research in Education (CFRE) at Keele University. His research teaching and development work focus mainly in areas associated with vocational education, further education and training, initial teacher education, school-based and policy related matters. Recent publications include *Training and its Alternatives* (1991) OU Press, *Truancy: the Politics of Compulsory Schooling* (1992) OU Press.

Derek Glover was educated at Luton Grammar School, London School of Economics and University of London Institute of Education. Taught in Nottingham, Harrow and Swindon, and then for 18 years Head of Burford School and Community College, Oxfordshire — complete with boarding unit and 40 acre agricultural unit. Changed direction in 1989 to work as a Senior Research Fellow at Keele (Successful Schools Project) and as Research Associate at Leicester (Leverhulme Grant-Maintained Schools Project). Lectures in educational management and tutors for the Open University. He was awarded a PhD in 1992 following research into community perceptions of school effectiveness.

Peter Holly taught in schools in England for 16 years. In 1982 he joined the staff of the Schools Council — the national curriculum development agency — where he specialized in organizational development and evaluation. From 1984 to 1989 he was tutor in curriculum studies at the Cambridge Institute of Education, producing two texts on school improvement, *Towards the Effective School* (Basil Blackwell) and *The Developing School* (Falmer Press). For the last three years he has been an independent consultant working on both sides of the Atlantic. In the USA he is a consultant for, among others, the NEA, the Puget Sound Educational Consortium, and Schools for the Twenty-First Century in Washington State. He is now based in Louisville, Kentucky, where he has worked with the Gheens Academy for Professional Development and Jefferson County Public Schools. He is currently consulting with restructuring efforts in Iowa and Washington State, the last bastions, he says, of 'State-initiated as opposed to State-mandated reform'.

Jeffrey Jones is the County Inspector for Assessment and Appraisal for Hereford and Worcester. He was previously County Director of the National Curriculum and Assessment Programme and TVEI Curriculum Advisor. A former secondary school teacher, Dr Jones has published widely in the areas of assessment and appraisal.

Isobel Roberts is the Senior Inspector for Development for Hereford and Worcester. Her teaching career has been spent almost exclusively in the secondary sector. Before entering the Inspectorate, she was a deputy headteacher in a large urban comprehensive school. An English graduate, Isobel took a year out to complete a Master's Degree in Cross-Cultural Studies which involved an exploration both of Afro-Caribbean and Indo-British Literature. She also studied part-time with Lawrence Stenhouse to achieve a Master's Degree in Educational Research. A committed exponent of Action-research she is presently embarking upon a PhD which will examine the effect of whole school planning on the teaching and learning process in high schools.

Vincent Russel is the Evaluation Co-ordinator for Hereford and Worcester TVEI. Prior to joining TVEI in 1990 he held the post of Head of Business Studies at Joseph Chamberlain Sixth Form College in Birmingham. He is currently responsible for developing the Formative Evaluation Programme in Hereford and Worcester.

David Turrell is Deputy Director of Hereford and Worcester TVEI. Previously he was Deputy Headteacher at Frankley Community High School. His work within Hereford and Worcester has been mainly focused on educational management and the development of teaching and learning strategies.

Index